Distance in the Theatre
The Aesthetics of Audience Response

Theater and Dramatic Studies, No. 17

Bernard Beckerman, Series Editor

Brander Matthews Professor of Dramatic Literature
Columbia University in the City of New York

Other Titles in This Series

Distance in the Theatre
The Aesthetics of Audience Response

by
Daphna Ben Chaim

U·M·I Research Press

Ann Arbor / London

Produced and distributed by
UMI Research Press
an imprint of
University Microfilms Inc.
Ann Arbor, Michigan 48106

This book was originally written
as a dissertation under the name of
Darlene M. Daubert.

Library of Congress Cataloging in Publication Data

Ben Chaim, Daphna.
    Distance in the theatre.

    (Theater and dramatic studies ; no. 17)
    Revision of thesis—University of Iowa, 1981.
    Bibliography: p.
    Includes index.
    1. Theater audiences—Psychological aspects. 2. Theater—
History—20th century. 3. Aesthetics, Modern. I. Title.
II. Series.

PN1590.A9B46   1984   792'.01'9   83-24231
ISBN 0-8357-1940-5 (pbk.)

to Paul and Karlyn Campbell

Contents

Introduction

I don't peep on sex. That's gone forever. You follow me? When my twigs happen to shall I say rest their peep on sexual conjugations, however periphrastic, I see only whites of eyes, so close, they glut me, no distance possible, and when you can't keep the proper distance between yourself and others, when you can no longer maintain an objective relation to matter, the game's not worth the candle, so forget it and remember that what is obligatory to keep in your vision is space, space in moonlight particularly, and lots of it.

—Harold Pinter, *No Man's Land,* Act I

Spooner is not a dramatic theorist and yet the terms, and the concepts, he employs—which Pinter expects his audience to comprehend—are those more common to philosophers than to fictional characters in plays. Speaking to Hirst, Spooner suggests that the proper relation between himself and sexuality (and, more generally, other persons) is characterized by "distance"; if he "can no longer maintain an objective relation to matter"—resist empathy, identification, loss of self—then he will not play. Involvement is "gone forever," not because he lacks capacity for involvement (otherwise he would not be glutted, "no distance possible," when he peeps "on sexual conjugations") but because he lacks capacity to maintain "distance." The quotation makes clear that in the twentieth century, most especially since the writings of Edward Bullough and Bertolt Brecht, the concept of "distance" in the sense that Spooner uses it has moved into the public domain.

Many dramatic theorists have suggested that a fundamental difference between reality and drama is that the psychological protection from the event is a condition of our experience in the theatre. Our involvement as audience members—the reason we peep—is an involvement of a special sort. We may cry when Desdemona is smothered to death, but we do not run onstage to save her. We may be shocked when the Duchess of Malfi is presented with what she thinks are the dead bodies of her husband and children, yet we perceive ironies, images and thematic implications of the scene which she, were she a real human being, probably could not. Our engagement during the theatrical experience may be intense, but it is not the kind of engagement that occurs in life experience. The difference is a function of distance.

The concept of "distance" has become quite central to both theatre practice and dramatic theory in the twentieth century, especially since the influential work of Bertolt Brecht. The concept is usually related to some quality, component, or perspective in the spectator's perception of the theatrical event. Since most theorists agree that the spectator's involvement is a crucial dimension of theatrical art, the notion has important implications for explaining how theatre "works," how it creates a particular experience.

Although major dramatic theorists today—J.L. Styan, Bernard Beckerman, Eric Bentley—agree that distance is fundamental to "the audience equation," they approach the problem from such different orientations, with such different goals, that a unified theory of distance is not easily found. There have been few attempts to analyze the phenomenon systematically, still fewer attempts to develop a complete theory for it, and, of course, little agreement as to what such a theory might be. In fact, different theorists apply the term "distance" to widely varying concepts, and in the work of a single theorist— even in a single passage—the term may be used inconsistently. It is the purpose of this book to examine the major dramatic, aesthetic, and philosophical conceptions of distance, and to discover in what ways, if any, these may contribute to a unified theory. If such a project creates a space between ourselves and the phenomenon itself, perhaps it will also allow for "a more objective relation to [the] matter."

The first chapter quickly surveys some of the more important ideas, from Shaftesbury to Bullough, on the subjects of disinterestedness and distance to identify a characteristic of our relation to art that has been observed by theorists since Aristotle. The chapter deals primarily with Bullough's argument as the first—and still the only systematic—attempt to explain the phenomenon. The purpose of this examination of Bullough is twofold: it permits me to describe the objections to theories of distance and it raises questions about the theories that need to be answered.

Chapter 2 analyzes the ideas of Jean-Paul Sartre concerning distance in the theatre. Like Bullough, Sartre is concerned with a description of the psychology of the phenomenon, the nature of the relationship between the art object and the perceiver. Chapters 3 and 4 examine the ideas of those theorists concerned with the techniques of the practical theatre and how these can be used to manipulate the spectator's psychological relationship to the theatrical event. Chapter 3 examines Bertolt Brecht's concept of alienation and its implications for a general theory of distance. Chapter 4 treats the theories of Antonin Artaud and Jerzy Grotowski, writers who ostensibly challenge the entire notion of aesthetic distance but, I believe, provide useful refinements of the theory. Chapter 5 considers the writings of film theorists Christian Metz and André Bazin, whose discussions of distance in that medium provide additional insights into the general concept and its particular applications in theatre. The concept of aesthetic distance has been applied by theorists in all art forms (it would not be an aesthetic theory if this were not possible). It is not my interest or desire to study the phenomenon of or the theories concerning distance in all of art, but because the relationship of film to theatre has troubled film theorists, and because the distinctions they draw often and largely turn on concepts of distance, I believe that the thinking of two notable film theorists may be especially useful. In the final chapter I attempt to define and assess our present understanding of the concept of distance, and point to the most fundamental principles that appear to be operating in the phenomenon of aesthetic distance.

1

The Concept of Psychical Distance

Dramatic theorists and theatre practitioners characterize distance in the theatre in a variety of ways, though nearly all assume that it concerns the spectator's psychological relation to the theatrical event. Concern with the state of mind, or mode of perception, of the spectator is perhaps the single unvarying feature in the entire history of the idea. As a theoretical concept, distance evolved from the concept of "aesthetic disinterestedness," present in Aristotle, but further articulated by several eighteenth-century British thinkers.[1] Lord Shaftesbury drew attention to disinterested perception in the art experience when he maintained that through "disinterestedness," a nonutilitarian concern with an object, selfishness is transcended. According to Shaftesbury, the virtue in aesthetic perception is that it is concerned with "no other than the love of order and beauty." It implies no desire to possess or use the object, nor to relate the object to any purpose other than perceiving it.[2] The involvement Shaftesbury describes is of a "pure" sort, devoid of any personal interest, desire, or motivation.

Shaftesbury's notion was widely accepted in subsequent British thought, especially by such theorists as Addison, Hutcheson, and Alison, and most notably by Edmund Burke in his theory of beauty and the sublime.[3] The idea received its most influential treatment in 1790 by Immanuel Kant in his *Critique of Judgement,* which explains how aesthetic judgment is possible. Kant maintains that all aesthetic judgments are particular, subjective judgments but devoid of any personal stake. He distinguishes the experience of the beautiful from that of the pleasant and the good on this basis.

> Both the Agreeable and the Good involve a reference to the faculty of desire, and are thus attended, the former with a delight pathologically conditioned (by stimuli), the latter with a pure practical delight. Such delight is determined not merely by the representation of the object, but also by the represented bond of connexion between the Subject and the real existence of the object. It is not merely the object, but also its real existence, that pleases. On the other hand the judgement of taste is simply *contemplative,* i.e. it is a judgement which is indifferent as to the existence of an object, and only decides how its character stands with the feeling of pleasure and displeasure. But not even is this contemplation itself directed to

concepts; for the judgement of taste is not a cognitive judgement (neither a theoretical one nor a practical), and hence, also, is not *grounded* on concepts, not yet *intentionally directed* to them.[4]

The experience of the pleasant and the good are both concerns for the satisfaction of our desires (the first a product of conditioning, the second a product of reasoning) and with the actual existence of the object represented. An aesthetic response, on the other hand, does not require that the represented object exist nor that the experience produce concepts. Instead, the concern is exclusively with the art object: not its source, its benefits, or its intellectual value.

> Of all these kinds of delight [the pleasant, the good, and the beautiful], that of taste in the beautiful may be said to be the one and only disinterested and *free* delight; for, with it, no interest, whether of sense or reason, extorts approval.[5]

Kant's explanation of disinterestedness has been enormously influential in aesthetics. Since the eighteenth century, the concept has become central to many philosophies, influencing, for instance, Schopenhauer's idea of "pure, will-less contemplation,"[6] and Henri Bergson's theory of comic laughter.[7]

However, while it has come to be generally agreed that Kant's concept of disinterestedness speaks to something true to our experience of art, finding the correct analysis of that experience has continued to trouble theorists. A generation after Kant, Samuel Taylor Coleridge (a Kantian) was already trying to reconcile concepts of the "disinterestedness" of aesthetic experience, on the one hand, with the desire for pleasure which art fulfills on the other.

> I would trace ["the *origin* of metre"] to the balance in the mind effected by that spontaneous effort which strives to hold in check the workings of passion. It might be easily explained likewise in what manner this salutary antagonism is assisted by the very state, which it counteracts; and how this balance of antagonists became organized into *metre* ... by a supervening act of the will and judgement, consciously and for the foreseen purpose of pleasure.[8]

And a generation after Coleridge, Friedrich Nietzsche used this apparent contradiction to mock Kant's formulation.

> "That is beautiful," says Kant, "which pleases without interesting." Without interesting! Compare this definition with this other one, made by a real "spectator" and "artist"—by Stendhal, who once called the beautiful *une promess de bonheur.* Here, at any rate, the one point which Kant makes prominent in the aesthetic position is repudiated and eliminated—*le désinteressement.* Who is right, Kant or Stendhal? When, forsooth, our aesthetes never get tired of throwing into the scales in Kant's favour the fact that under the magic of beauty men can look at even naked female statues "without interest," we can certainly laugh a little at their expense: ... Pygmalion was not necessarily an "unaesthetic man."[9]

As Nietzsche's criticism suggests, Kant's formulation has long since come to seem too restrictive and reductive; there are surely some senses in which art is both a personal matter and a matter of self-interest.

Psychical Distance

It was precisely this issue that Edward Bullough attempted to resolve early in the twentieth century in his famous essay, "'Psychical Distance' as a Factor in Art and an Aesthetic Principle," in which he initiated a new line of thinking.[10]

> Distance does not imply an impersonal, purely intellectually interested relation. . . . On the contrary, it describes a *personal* relation, often highly emotionally coloured, but *of a peculiar character*. Its peculiarity lies in that the personal character of the relation has been, so to speak, filtered. It has been cleared of the practical, concrete nature of its appeal, without, however, thereby losing its original constitution.[11]

Bullough argues that personal interest retains its essential character in the art experience even while, purified of practical motives, it has been transformed into disinterestedness. Whereas Kant has asserted that "the judgement of taste cannot rest on any subjective end as its ground,"[12] Bullough tries to show a way in which this is at once true and not true.

The mechanism by which personal interest is disconnected from the practical is what Bullough calls "distance."[13] This, he makes clear, is a psychological phenomenon that in his view is independent of, and prior to, the spectator's awareness of fiction.

> Events and characters of the drama . . . appeal to us like persons and incidents of normal experience, except that that side of their appeal, which would usually affect us in a directly personal manner, is held in abeyance. This difference . . . is generally explained by reference to the knowledge that the characters and situations are "unreal," imaginary. . . . But, as a matter of fact, the "assumption" upon which the imaginative emotional reactions is based in not necessarily the condition, but often the consequence, of Distance: that is to say, the converse of the reason usually stated would then be true: vis. that Distance, by changing our relation to the characters, renders them seemingly fictitious, not that the fictitiousness of the characters alters our feelings towards them. It is, of course, to be granted that the actual and admitted unreality of the dramatic action reinforces the effects of Distance. (pp. 91-92)

According to Bullough, distance, an independent mental force, operates in two ways. First of all, distance functions in a "negative, inhibitory" way: the mental force inserts itself between our practical self (with needs and desires) and our experience of the work. The artistic phenomenon, then, is put "out of gear with our practical, actual self [,] by allowing it to stand outside the context of our personal needs and ends" (p. 89). In addition to the inhibitory aspect, Bullough maintains that distance operates positively by permitting us to elaborate our experience on the "new basis created by the inhibitory action of Distance" (p. 89).

Bullough maintains that distance is an essential characteristic of the perception of art, though the effect is variable:

> That all art requires a Distance-limit beyond which, and a Distance within which only, aesthetic appreciation becomes possible, is the *psychological formulation of a general characteristic of Art,* viz. its *anti-realistic* nature. (pp. 98-99)

Bullough is maintaining that distance is intrinsic to our perception of all of art, something without which the work of art, or its perception as a work of art, would not exist, a quality which can be emphasized or de-emphasized but not eliminated. According to Bullough, distance emphasizes the artistic aspects of the work of art—that is, how the art object differs from "ordinary" objects within the real world.

Bullough's formulation has appealed to many aestheticians because it reasserts the uniqueness of art[14] and of the mode of its perception—an aesthetic attitude.[15] Moreover, unlike Kant's "disinterestedness," Bullough's "distance" admits a personal interest in the work of art but one purified of any practical implications. In choosing the phrase "psychical distance," Bullough moves the discussion further toward the perceptual and psychological and away from the absolute attributes of the work of art itself, a shift congenial to contemporary philosophy and aesthetics.

Bullough's essay has been seminal: even its contradictions have generated theories. Although it has been quite significant to recent theorists—notably Susanne Langer, S.H. Butcher, Eliseo Vivas, J.L. Styan, Jerome Stolnitz, and others—few theorists have closely analyzed Bullough's theory. For example, in both *Philosophy in a New Key*[16] and *Feeling and Form,* Susanne Langer explains major tenets of Bullough's essay, specifically in regard to the perceiver's relation to the art work—personal but of a "peculiar character." Langer quotes Bullough at length, using his theory as a foundation for her own theory of illusion but quietly translating its basis from psychology to semiotics:

> This relation "of a peculiar character" is, I believe, our natural relation to a symbol that embodies an idea and presents it for our contemplation, not for practical action, but "cleared of the practical, concrete nature of its appeal." It is for the sake of this remove that art deals entirely in illusions, which, because of their lack of "practical, concrete nature," are readily distanced as symbolic forms.[17]

Langer does not attempt to explain why Bullough's conception is an adequate account of the psychological and perceptual phenomenon that occurs while viewing art, and more specifically, what role the psychological force of distance plays in the experience of illusion. Though she accepts Bullough's concept of distance as fundamental to illusion, Langer implicitly reverses the order of

Bullough's description: for Langer, "our natural relation to a symbol" (e.g., fictionality) precedes distance, whereas Bullough maintains that "this remove" from art is actually the result of distance.

Many theorists, in addition to Langer, have been influenced by Bullough, but few have thoroughly analyzed Bullough's concept of distance before selectively applying his ideas to their own theories.[18]

Bullough was the first to specifically define a conception of distance distinct from disinterestedness (a lack of personal interest);[19] but his explanations pose serious difficulties.

One of the major difficulties is with his contention that "distance" is a psychological force that "inserts" itself between our perception of the art work and a practical response, blocking the viewer's needs and interests:

> It is a difference in outlook, due ... to the insertion of Distance. This distance appears to lie between our own self and its affections, ... anything which affects our being, bodily or spiritually, e.g. as sensation, perception, emotional state or idea. (p. 89)

Distance thereby allows the art work "to stand outside the context of our personal needs and ends" so that the perceiver can look at it "objectively," interpreting any responses to the work as characteristics of the phenomenon and not as modes of his or her own being (p. 89). Bullough suggests here that although the practical self is not *completely* blocked by distance, the feelings that "come through" are perceived to be a part of the art work rather than subjective responses to the art work.

Though obviously something within the viewer's consciousness prevents a "practical" response, Bullough does not explain the psychological mechanism. He identifies it as such, but what it is and what initiates it he does not say. He explicitly rejects "fictionality," the awareness of the artificiality of the art work, as its cause, instead making fictionality a *product* of psychical distance. This has the unfortunate effect of requiring the existence of a complex and unexplained psychological force for which there is neither evidence nor, apparently, speculation in the psychological literature. Of course, it is precisely fictionality which provides a simple explanation for "a difference in outlook" that occurs when one attends to an art object; Bullough might have demonstrated the inadequacy of this simple explanation before attempting to provide a complex one. His claims that distance is an "essential characteristic" of the "aesthetic consciousness," "that special mental attitude towards, and outlook upon, experience, which finds its most pregnant expression in the various forms of Art" (p. 90), are unsupported by an explanation of what "triggers" this aesthetic attitude when confronted with art works, or what signals distance to "insert itself" when in the aesthetic attitude.

Bullough's account cannot explain how distance actually affects or determines the viewer's involvement with the art work. When he states that distance causes the viewer to observe the work "objectively," he seems to imply that a lack of direct emotional involvement exists, yet he still maintains that the viewer has a personal relation to the object. How this paradoxically involved-yet-removed relation to the art work occurs is not altogether clear. In other words, lacking an explanation of the psychological force, the psychological force explains nothing. Bullough's theory reduces to a perception of a paradox and an assertion that it can be resolved by psychology.

Bullough seems to mean by "objectivity" the attribution of one's own feelings to the object—a special form (without negative connotations) of what literary theorists call the pathetic fallacy. Thus the emotion is "objectified," literally distanced, by investment in something else; because it is not claimed as one's own it need not (nor can it) have a personal objective (purpose). But if this were the basic mechanism of distance—the disengaged personal emotion invested in the object—it would seem that Bullough would describe the "ideal" as the *greatest* amount of distance (emotion invested in the object), and yet he maintains that the ideal experience of the art work takes place when the viewer has the least amount of distance without losing it, the most intense personal experience without too much subjectivity, a basic principle which Bullough refers to as the "antinomy of Distance"—the "utmost decrease of Distance without its disappearance" (p. 94):

> The jealous spectator of Othello will indeed appreciate and enter into the play the more keenly, the greater the resemblance with his own experience—*provided* that he succeeds in keeping the Distance between the action of the play and his personal feelings: a very difficult performance in the circumstances. (p. 93)

It seems altogether correct to say that the jealous spectator may have a more intense experience than others when viewing Othello, identifying with the character as he simultaneously experiences intense emotions in relation to his own wife. Since the play appeals to issues of immediate concern to the spectator, it is only natural that his emotional response would be more intense than for other spectators. It is not clear, however, what Bullough means when he refers to a required degree of distance between the action of the play and the viewer's personal feelings, a required distance without which there can be no aesthetic experience. When is the spectator too personally involved to permit distance? Is the spectator under-distanced when he is not consciously aware of the characters of Othello and Desdemona and only thinks of his own personal relationship? Or when the intensity of his identification prevents his awareness of the formal qualities of the art object?

Such questions point to the incompleteness of Bullough's explanations, but also to the possibility that he may mean several different things by the word "distance." For instance, and despite his explicit rejection of fictionality as a cause of Distance, in the passage above Bullough implies that distance is an awareness of the work as fiction. The distance required for the jealous spectator would in fact be an awareness that the events are represented in a play. With this explanation, it is understandable that Bullough calls for the greatest reduction of distance "without its disappearance." It seems that Bullough wants viewers to remember that they are viewing a work of art which is invested with emotions that the *viewer* projects into the fictional characters and feels *pseudo-vicariously.*

In one sense, then, Bullough means by distance an emotional dissociation by the spectator from his emotion, the attribution of his own feelings to something outside himself. In another sense he seems to mean some level of awareness by the spectator that his engagement is with a virtual object. The difference is vast, as can be seen by the kinds of theatrical practice that these understandings would seem to encourage: on the one hand, an intensification of emotional involvement, empathy, with the characters (as in realistic plays); on the other, an intensification of awareness of the fictionality of the whole, alienation (as in Brecht's Epic Theatre).

This contradiction is left unresolved by Bullough; unaware of it, he stressed one direction of his thinking in the first part and the other in the latter part of the essay. And, as will be seen subsequently, it is precisely the first which Sartre develops and the second which Brecht emphasizes. While Bullough speaks vaguely of a balance, or limits within which distance must operate if the object is to be seen as a work of art, his difficulty is not merely in defining those limits but more fundamentally lies in defining the notion of distance itself.

The problems of definition are compounded when Bullough seems to confuse distance as a characteristic of the spectator's experience (which is his theoretical stance, as when he describes it as a psychological force), with suggestions that it is characteristic of the art object (which emerges primarily when he is speaking critically). For instance, he says that " 'Under-distancing' is the commonest failing of the *subject,* an excess of Distance is a frequent failing of the Art" (p. 94). I take it that he means by this that failures in the art experience caused by under- or over-distancing are generally produced either by the spectator's excessive involvement (for whatever reason), or by the inaccessibility of the work to the spectator (for whatever reason); but what he *says* is that the work manifests an excess of distance. This well illustrates the phenomenon which he associates with distance, that the perceiver attributes his perception to the object! And it illustrates further the difficulty of the kind of "phenomenological reduction" that is required of a philosopher who wishes to talk about art. The very thinker who proposes a theory based on the distinction between the spectator's acknowledged and unacknowledged feelings toward an object cannot keep the matter straight. Clearly, when one describes a work of art as artificial, precious, bombastic, etc.—characterizations which might be used by a spectator who believes a work to manifest an excess of distance— these high level descriptions imply perceptions of an art object which contain evaluative components, and this spectator could, in turn, be described as over-distanced. But one cannot describe the art works themselves as over-distanced without significantly altering the meaning of the concept.

There is still other evidence in his essay that Bullough means several things when he speaks of distance. One of the most troublesome ambiguities appears in his attempt to more particularly define the principles that set the limits within which psychical distance must operate; that is, what produces under-distancing and what produces over-distancing. As noted above, Bullough cites the case of a jealous husband at a production of *Othello* as an example of under-distancing, but even there Bullough makes his position clear that the most effective art experience is one in which distance is reduced to the greatest extent possible without its elimination. That being so, it is difficult to see how that principle is operating when he asserts that the effectiveness of Greek tragedy results from the increased distance produced by temporal remoteness.

> Our understanding of Greek tragedy suffers admittedly under our inability to revert to the point of view for which it was originally written.... [However,] provided the distance is not too wide, the result of its intervention has everywhere been to enhance the *art*-character of such works and to lower their original ethical and social force of appeal. (p. 103)

Bullough is here suggesting that Greek tragedy is effective today because its temporal remoteness has reduced or eliminated potential practical responses to the work, that is, concern for current social and political issues addressed in the play. Because the issues no longer directly apply to the twentieth century or must be metaphorically inferred, the spectator is better able to appreciate the tragedy as "art." However, if this radical reduction in personal involvement enhances the "*art*-character" of the work, then is personal involvement an essential component in the aesthetic experience at all? Indeed, here Bullough seems to imply a reversion to the traditional, or Kantian, position that the aesthetic experience in its essence is disinterested. Bullough's critical perceptions that Greek tragedy is seen today differently than it was by its contemporaries and that this temporal "distance" in some manner enhances some qualities of the experience of plays seem incontrovertibly true, but his interpretations of these perceptions raise questions about what he conceives the aesthetic experience to be and how he defines distance.

Whereas early in the essay Bullough calls for a reduction of distance without its disappearance, when discussing tragedy he seems to diminish the role of personal involvement, claiming that it prevents the spectator from a genuine experience of the "tragic" as opposed to the "merely sad."

> Tragedy is not sad; if it were, there would indeed be little sense in its existence. For the tragic is just in so far different from the merely sad, as it is distanced; and it is largely the exceptional which produces the Distance of tragedy: exceptional situations, exceptional characters, exceptional destinies and conduct.... Tragedy trembles always on the knife-edge of a

personal reaction, and sympathy which finds relief in tears tends almost always towards a loss of Distance. Such a loss naturally renders tragedy unpleasant to a degree: it becomes sad, dismal, harrowing, depressing. But real tragedy . . . truly appreciated is not sad. (pp. 103-4)

Previously the word "personal" was used to indicate the location of a subjective response but here Bullough seems to use the word to indicate a quality: "personal" has biographical implications, suggesting that the feelings partly derive from one's own history and experience (as in the *Othello* example). When Bullough applauds the increase of distance in viewing Greek tragedy, he claims that its effectiveness is partially due to its remoteness from the spectator's "personal" life.

Although not clearly explaining when too much or too little distance exists, Bullough emphatically maintains that distance is inherent to all art (p. 90).

That all art requires a Distance-limit beyond which, and a Distance within which only, aesthetic appreciation becomes possible, is the *psychological formulation of a general characteristic of Art,* viz. *its anti-realistic nature.* . . . To say that Art is anti-realistic simply insists upon the fact that Art is not nature, never pretends to be nature and strongly resists any confusion with nature. It emphasizes the *art*-character of Art: "artistic" is synonymous with "anti-realistic"; it explains even sometimes a very marked degree of artificiality. (pp. 98-99)

The interesting point here is not simply that Bullough considers distance to be an important factor in all art, but, more importantly, he implies that distance has very much to do with our awareness of the object *as* art ("it never pretends to be nature"). Because art is not nature but artificially created by human beings, we remain aware of its art-character. Its very "anti-realistic nature" appears to be a determining factor of distance.

Bullough specifically deals with this notion of the art-character of the object in relation to theatre. He considers the "bodily vehicle" of drama to be a considerable risk to distance: its use of real objects and real people within actual space could blur the perceiver's awareness of the art-character of the event, its artificiality. "To counterbalance a confusion with nature," Bullough explains that other features of the theatrical presentation increase our awareness of theatre as art—the stage, costumes, artificial light, make-up, etc.

Bullough's emphasis on the artificiality of the theatrical conventions and their importance in relation to distance foreshadows the views of Antonin Artaud and Bertolt Brecht, who both share this crucial principle in their otherwise apparently opposed theories. The positions of both theorists will be discussed in subsequent chapters.

Bullough's essay is shot through with concern for the awareness of the "art-character," or fictionality, of a work of art; every instance of distance that he cites involves a perception of unreality. Yet, as noted, he specifically rejects knowledge of the fictionality of the object as the cause for the phenomenon of distance.

> One of the best-known examples [of distance] is to be found in our attitude toward the events and characters of drama: they appeal to us like persons..., except that... which would usually affect us in a directly personal manner, is held in abeyance. This difference, so well known as to be almost trivial, is generally explained by references to the knowledge that the characters and situations are "unreal," imaginary.... But, as a matter of fact, the "assumption" upon which the imaginative emotional reaction is based is not necessarily the condition, but often the consequence of Distance; that is to say, the converse of the reason usually stated would then be true: viz. that Distance, by changing our relation to the characters renders them seemingly fictitious, not that the fictitiousness of the characters alters our feelings towards them. It is, of course, to be granted that the actual and admitted unreality of the dramatic action reinforces the effects of Distance.... The proof of the seeming paradox that it is Distance which primarily gives to dramatic action the appearance of unreality and not vice versa, is the observation that the same filtration of our sentiments and the same seeming "unreality" of *actual* men and things occur, when at times, by a sudden change of inward perspective, we are overcome by the feeling that "all the world's a stage." (pp. 91-92)

I quote so fully here because it is in this passage that the issues most crucial to Bullough's essay and also to this book are most nearly confronted; and it is from this passage that some essential distinctions may be made regarding the specific focus of this study. For it is clear that Bullough's ambition is to deal with a psychological phenomenon which, in his view, would exist whether there were art objects or not (as, for instance, in the fog anecdote at the beginning of the essay) and, moreover, with an "aesthetic attitude" which is not directly related to any particular artistic medium nor even to a particular work of art. Both of these more general psychological conditions may arguably exist, but it is the assumption of this book that the phenomenon of distance can be analyzed and understood in dramatic art independently of them. In fact, it is my contention that such a limited scope is useful for greater precision of analysis. Indeed, it seems likely that the larger subjects of Bullough's interest might be best understood in an extensive examination of distance within the limited scope of a single art form. At least, if that were known it would be easier to isolate any unresolved components of the experience.

Bullough's larger purpose, in which he wants to confront the psychological phenomenon of the "seeming 'unreality' of *actual* men and things" in the real world, requires that he reject the perceived artificiality of art as a cause of distance. But he is thereby required to make the implausible assertion that distance *causes* art to be perceived as unreal, and further, that this unreality reinforces the unreality of distance. It also forces him into what is an even more serious difficulty, that this "sudden change of inward perspective," which is the perception of unreality, appears causeless; it merely strikes us, like lightning or grace. Though Bullough establishes with considerable descriptive skill the conditions of a shipboard fog in which "the transformation by Distance" puts the actual world "out of gear with our practical, actual self," he does not appear to understand them as *conditions* at all. Instead he speaks of distance as "emerging with startling suddenness, ... like a momentary switching on of some new current." If distancing cannot be attributed to any external stimuli, then why is the phenomenon so commonly associated with art objects? Bullough's failure to treat this crucial question makes the more limited purview of this book necessary.

2

A Voluntary Act

Like Bullough, who attempts to descriptively analyze our psychological relation to art works, Jean-Paul Sartre is concerned with the fundamental psychological conditions of aesthetic experiences. Sartre suggests his conception of distance in his attempts to distinguish between imaging and perceiving. To illustrate the distinction Sartre cites the example of the actress Franconay impersonating Maurice Chevalier. He contends that we *perceive* the impersonator (small, stout, female body), then shift our consciousness, thereby *imaging* the nonexistent object, "Maurice Chevalier":

> The result is that the imitation is but an approximation. The object produced by Franconay by means of her body is a feeble form which can always be interpreted in two distinct ways: I am always free to see Maurice Chevalier as an image, or a small woman who is making faces. [1]

Sartre maintains that, when faced with a live performance in a theatre whereby human beings are representing nonexistent characters (or, in the case of Chevalier, an existent but absent human being), we must shift back and forth between perceiving and imaging, but he does admit that at times the continual "gliding" back and forth results in a kind of momentary synthesis:

> The imagined synthesis is accompanied by a fully spontaneous consciousness and, we might even say, one that is fully free. This is so because only a formal will can prevent consciousness from gliding from the level of the image to that of the perception. In most cases this gliding occurs all the same, from time to time. It even happens quite often that the synthesis is not completely made: the face and body of the impersonator do not lose their individuality; but the expressive something "Maurice Chevalier" nevertheless appears on that face, on that female body. A hybrid condition follows, which is altogether neither perception nor image, which should be described by itself. These unstable and momentary states evidently supply the spectator with the most pleasant aspects of imitation. This is no doubt due to the fact that the relationship of the object to the material of the imitation is here one of *possession*. The absent Maurice Chevalier chose the body of a woman to make his appearance. (p. 40)

Sartre here maintains that during such in-between states, we neither perceive nor image completely, but see a quality of the object "Maurice Chevalier" *on* the body of Franconay.

Sartre's distinction between the image and the perception follows the lead of Husserl in maintaining that perceptions are passive syntheses (taking place through association within time), whereas images are active syntheses, essentially creative. Sartre agrees with Husserl that the difference between images and perceptions quite naturally results from the difference in their "fundamental structure of intentional syntheses," but finds this explanation incomplete, contending that not only is the intentionality different, but the matter itself must also be different.[2] He goes on to make that distinction between the two, maintaining that perceiving is neither a voluntary nor a spontaneous process but a gradual acquiring of knowledge as we observe objects (pp. 9-10), whereas imaging, on the other hand, is spontaneous.[3] In addition, "the image teaches nothing: it is organized exactly like the objects which do produce knowledge, but it is complete at the very moment of its appearance." No matter how long we may look at the image, we will never find anything there that we did not put there. The image is characterized by an "essential poverty": it has no relationship with the rest of the world (pp. 10-11). The primary distinction between the image and the perception that Sartre makes is that perception posits its object as existing whereas the image posits its object as either nonexistent or absent (p. 16).

In other words, the image, which is a relationship between object and consciousness, involves a negation of the world: the object of consciousness is nonexistent. Because the object of perception is existent, and that of the image is nonexistent, Sartre claims that imaging and perceiving must exclude each other (p. 171). Therefore, we cannot perceive and image at the same time. "The formation of an imaginative consciousness is accompanied ... by an annihilation of a perceptual consciousness, and vice versa" (pp. 171-72). Sartre contends, therefore, that if we are viewing a painting, so long as we are viewing the canvas and the frame in and of themselves, the aesthetic object will not appear. The aesthetic object "will appear at the moment when consciousness, undergoing a radical change in which the world is negated, will itself become imaginative" (p. 274).

This distinction between imaging and perceiving relates to the concept of distance in a fundamental way: for Sartre, we are aesthetically distanced when we are imaginatively experiencing the image as opposed to when we are perceiving the real. Distance occurs when the real is negated:

> For a consciousness to be able to imagine it must be able to escape from the world by its very nature, it must be able by its own efforts to withdraw from the world. In a word it must be free. Thus the thesis of unreality has yielded us the possibility of negation as its condition. (p. 267)

Only by holding the real world at a distance, negating it, freeing oneself from its reality criterion, can consciousness, in Sartre's view, experience the image. In the case of the aesthetic object, because it is the referent of the image, it is nonactual, that is, nonexistent;[4] the aesthetic experience occurs only when perception ceases, when the viewer shifts from the perceptual attitude of consciousness to the imaginative.

Sartre's concept of exclusive states of consciousness in the pragmatic and aesthetic attitudes is illustrated by the viewing of a painting of Charles VIII:

> As long as we observe the canvas and the frame for themselves the esthetic object "Charles VIII" will not appear. It is not that it is hidden by the picture, but because it cannot present itself to a realizing consciousness. It will appear at the moment when consciousness, undergoing a radical change in which the world is negated, will itself become imaginative. This Charles VIII on the canvas is necessarily the correlative of the intentional act of an imaginative consciousness. And since this Charles VIII, who is an unreality so long as he is grasped on the canvas, is precisely the object of our esthetic appreciations (it is he who "moves" us, who is "painted with intelligence, power, and grace," etc.), we are led to recognize that, in a picture, the esthetic object is something unreal....That which is real...are the results of the brush strokes, the stickiness of the canvas, its grain, the polish spread over the colors. But all this does not constitute the object of esthetic appreciation. What is "beautiful" is something which cannot be experienced as a perception and which, by its very nature, is out of the world....The painting should then be conceived as a material thing *visited* from time to time (every time that the spectator assumes the imaginative attitude) by an unreal which is precisely the *painted object.* (pp. 274-75)

The aesthetic experience, in Sartre's view, involves a radical shift from perceiving to imaging; we may perceive the real brush strokes, canvas, and colors that exist within the real world, but only when we permit ourselves to imagine the nonexistent do we experience the aesthetic object.

Sartre's concept of distance for theatre is dependent on his theory of the imagination, in that he sees theatre as a negation of reality in the same way that the image is a negation of the world.

> We must realize that a dramatic representation has a perfectly illusory character, but in that case as its structure is unreal, it is for this very quality that we have to exploit it, as the negation of reality...and not as an imitation of it.[5]

For Sartre, the theatrical event is always symbolic, for "the real serves to create unreality."[6] Because the event is a negation of reality, the event reveals, in Sartre's terms, its own absence.

> The event represented itself reveals its *absence,* for it happened a long time ago or never existed, and reality dissolves into pure appearance. Yet these false appearances reveal to us the true laws governing human behavior.[7]

Conceiving theatre as existing fundamentally in the realm of the imaginary, and its represented events revealing the absence of their reality, Sartre is actually quite close to Bullough's position in radically distinguishing perception of reality and unreality (but Sartre calls only the former an act of perception).

When Sartre refers to theatre (and the image) as a negation of reality, he seems to mean that the essential elements of the theatrical performance are not the actual but the nonexistent characters, events, and places. The significance of the event occurs in the spectator's imagination: it is only the viewer, in his imagination, who experiences the nonexistent fictional world. So when Sartre says that "reality dissolves into pure appearance," he is suggesting that the real actors, scenery and props have merely become the vehicle for the unreal world of the play, and because the theatrical production openly reveals itself as representation, it acknowledges the "absence" of what is represented: "the real serves to create unreality."

Sartre seems to mean that distance has to do with the spectator's experience of the real world as the representation of the nonexistent imaginary world. Since Sartre views imagining as a negation of the world, increased distance for Sartre means increased imaginative involvement—an intense experience of the image (the negation of reality) with little awareness of the perception of reality. In *Saint Genet*, Sartre tells an anecdote about how Genet as a child was compelled to give up a knife that he found. Genet discovered that the loss was a gain, because the knife—and the dragons that he slew with it— were more real to his imagination when it was *only* real to his imagination, because then his mind wholly possessed it.[8]

Sartre explains the power that an image may have, how it can be possessed and yet in a sense possess a mind, as deriving from emotion. Emotion for Sartre has a magical potency, it is "an abrupt drop of consciousness into the magical."[9] What is magical about emotion is that it can confer a kind of belief in an object or in an unreal image or in an image that is made from the object:

> True emotion . . . is accompanied by belief. The qualities conferred upon objects are taken as true qualities. Exactly what is meant by that? Roughly this: the emotion is undergone. One cannot abandon it at will; it exhausts itself, but we cannot stop it. Besides, the behavior which boils down to itself alone does nothing else than sketch upon the object the emotional quality which we confer upon it.[10]

The emotion is ours and therefore so are the qualities (the image) that we confer upon the object. Projecting our emotions into the image produces the semblance of belief in it, yet it is a belief that is dependent on our prior act of will to imagine, and therefore it is a conditional belief, which can be withdrawn if or when the emotion ceases to exist.[11] In other words, belief is a necessary accompaniment of emotion but its object may be real and therefore involuntary or it may be an image and therefore initially voluntary. But emotion becomes a kind of spell that traps the will—so long as it lasts.

In his story about Genet, Sartre suggests that the young Genet had three levels of "belief" in his knife: when he had removed the rust so that it shone;

when, after it had been taken from him, he scraped a stick into a knife-form; and then, after even that was taken from him, when he depended wholly on his imagination. The significance of the story is that at each step he discovered that the knife was more completely in his possession (or vice-versa). This, I think, is what Sartre means by *increased* distance, that there is the least possible impediment to the imagination after it is stimulated by the object.

If increased distance for Sartre is the increased imaginative involvement in the unreal, with a minimal awareness of reality, it may initially seem confusing that Sartre characterizes theatre as manifesting "absolute distance":

> I think that the real origin, the real meaning of the theatre is to put the world of men at an absolute distance, an impassable distance, the distance separating me from the stage. The actor is so distant that I can see him but will never be able to touch him or act upon him.[12]

For Sartre the physical distance separating audience from performers becomes a metaphor for the psychological/emotional protection of the spectator. It is not the human being (who is acting) that cannot be touched, but the "actor" (as character). The rules of the game, the theatrical conventions, create a barrier that can be destroyed but not reached across.

Sartre considers this psychological removal as the first phase of a theatrical experience: the distanced viewers come to realize that the characters they are imagining embody aspects of themselves.

> In the theatre, we remain outside and the hero meets his fate before our eyes. But the impact on us and our feelings is all the stronger in that the hero is also ourselves, even if outside us.[13]

This is the paradoxical state that interested Bullough: the projection of the spectator's own feelings into an object only on condition of an "absolute distance"—the assurance of the separation of the self from the imagined object:

> Exploiting a contradiction: the man presented is myself, but without power over myself. That is, making us discover ourselves as *others,* as if people were looking at us; in other words, achieving an objectivity which I cannot get from my reflection.[14]

The impact is supposedly stronger "in that the hero is also ourselves, even if outside us." Because the viewer is psychologically protected from the characters and events onstage, knowing that they are separate from him or her, the spectator can permit the play to lead him or her into a closer scrutiny of self.

Conceiving "absolute distance" as fundamental to theatre, Sartre demonstrates his debt to Bertolt Brecht when he suggests that we should not attempt to decrease distance but should exploit it,[15] but Sartre rejects what he considers the over-distancing of Brecht's Epic Theatre. Though Sartre wants emotions to be at a certain distance, he does not believe in destroying identification. Like Bullough, Sartre thinks the two—identification with the hero and distance from the events onstage—should exist simultaneously:

> If you want to make an audience understand what returning from a war and remembering that one has committed atrocities in it means, you have to make the audience identify with your hero. It must take *him* as an incentive to *its own self-hatred.*[16]

To achieve critical understanding, Sartre thinks it essential to create a critical perspective *through* the spectator's identification with the hero: the spectator projects his or her own feelings into the character only to discover a hatred of self as a hatred of the characters' actions in war. Though Sartre uses the term "distance" and aligns himself with Brecht, he obviously conceives of theatre and its use of distance in a very different way, one *requiring* identification to have effect.

Sartre considers the "need for distancing the object to some extent by displacing it in time and space" as "an aesthetic requirement of theatre."[17] To be imaginatively involved in the representation of the unreal, to the point where the spectator can emotionally invest in the object outside him or herself, the event needs to be removed from the viewer in order that the intense personal emotions (in response to one's own immediate life) not interfere with absorption in the experience of the events onstage.

When Sartre calls for an increase of distance in the theatre—an "exploitation" of distance—he certainly does not mean an increased awareness of the "*art*-character" of the object (in Bullough's sense of distance), nor does he conceive of increased distance as a highly conscious, critical mental state (in Brecht's sense), but conceives of increased distance as an intense involvement in the representation. For though he assumes that "absolute distance" is a necessary condition, what he values in art is a negation of self in the oblivion of a vicarious existence which is, at least at that moment, the destruction of distance.

This explains why, for Sartre, the actor directly addressing the audience causes the imaginary character to disappear, thereby destroying the spectator's distanced involvement.

> In the theatre the "someone else" never looks at me; or should he happen to look at me, then the actor, the imaginary character, vanishes. Hamlet or Volpone vanishes and it is Barrault or Dullin looking at me. What is wrong with addressing an audience is that it causes the imaginary character to vanish and to be replaced by the presence of the real person.[18]

Sartre contends that aesthetic distance is destroyed when the spectator becomes aware of the real as only real, the actor as actor and not as nonexistent being in the spectator's imagination. The awareness of the real as real is not what Sartre finds most valuable or most intrinsic to the art experience.

Whatever destroys distance, and thus the spectator's imaginative engagement with the unreal, does not, therefore, serve art's highest function.

Sartre's conception of distance as involvement in the unreal is consistent with his view that empathy is a necessary consequence of distance, for if that involvement consists of imagining a world, a society, characters, and the thoughts and feelings of characters which are actually the projections of the spectator who is imagining (though guided by the work of art), then it is some part of himself that the spectator is unconsciously responding to in the fiction. Sartre suggests that there is a fundamental psychological paradox in which real confrontations create the need for a protective distance while the prior existence of a condition of protective distance permits vulnerability. He suggests that one's selfhood is in some manner threatened by direct contact with another human being, which requires one to erect a defensive barrier. But the averted eyes of a fictional character—neither from the page nor the stage does the character "look at me"—permits one to be an observer and therefore to merge imaginatively with the character's point of view. The extreme of this phenomenon, Sartre says, is the theatre where the character in the real body of an actor may gaze in my direction without "looking at me"; yet if the actor's eyes do seem to focus on me, then at that moment Hamlet disappears from my imagination and I am being uncomfortably confronted by Barrault.

With his focus on the imagination, and his conception of distance as the difference between the real and the unreal, with distance being an intense engagement with the unreal (with minimal perception of the real), it is understandable why Sartre finds such theatrical events as the "happening" or the "documentary play" ("theatre of fact") so disturbing. For Sartre, they deny the "absolute distance" fundamental to theatre because they rely too heavily on reality.

> A happening is real. It exists and it gives an effective opportunity to certain kinds of mass reactions, which we can take as fact. The problem really is: what happens to the performance insofar as it is an appeal to the free imagination of the spectator? Is not this spontaneous bringing of something into being by means that are more or less cruel the very opposite of theatre, or rather is it not the moment when theatre destroys itself?[19]

Because the happening exploits the reality of the audience, Sartre considers it as endangering imaginative involvement. Though he does not actually claim that happenings completely destroy distance, Sartre does believe that they cause confusion in the spectator by jolting the viewer back and forth between increased distance and a near destruction of distance by vacillating between the near creation of illusion and the shattering of it with the intrusion of the real (the performance of actors) and the intrusion of reality (current issues within the world).[20]

This presumed confusion between the real and the unreal in the happening and the "theatre of fact" is what Sartre refers to as the "crisis of the imaginary" in the theatre. He maintains that in both the theatrical illusion is "absorbed or swallowed by some real and sadistic action imposed on the spectator,"[21] in both the limits of distance are tested.

Sartre's theories present a number of difficulties. In addition to those difficulties that are normally associated with getting "inside" the thought of a complex mind, Sartre's long career creates another. Though he seems in the majority of his works to explore the implications of his ideas rather than to evolve them, that work is of an extremely diverse nature: technical and popular philosophy, criticism, history, politics, sociology, etc. He does not always write with the same precision, nor are his theories always consistent. Also, he seems to deal with the experience of viewing theatre performances in a more ambiguous and complex manner when describing his actual experiences than he does on a more theoretical level. It seems to me, for instance, that his theoretical dichotomy of "perception" versus "imagination" is belied by his description of Franconay impersonating Maurice Chevalier. "The most pleasant aspects" of the experience, he says, involve neither imaging nor perceiving but a "hybrid condition," which seems to be essentially a tension between what is seen and what is imagined:

> It even happens quite often that the synthesis is not completely made: the face and body of the impersonator do not lose their individuality; but the expressive something "Maurice Chevalier" nevertheless appears on that face, on that female body. A hybrid condition follows, which is altogether neither perception nor image, which should be described by itself. These unstable and momentary states evidently supply the spectator with the most pleasant aspects of imitation. (p. 40)

Even his vocabulary, specifically in his use of the term "synthesis," brings Sartre's experience quite close to that described by Bullough; that is, the experience is neither an annihilation of the perceptual object nor a total awareness of the real, but a tension produced by an awareness of both.

The very distinction that Sartre wishes to make between "perception" and "imagination," the experience of the real versus the experience of the unreal, seems more commonsensical than true. Perception as it has been usually understood by philosophers and psychologists involves an imaginative component. Indeed, it might be argued that the survival benefit of imagination is that perception would be inadequate to cope with reality without it. This is more than a semantic problem with Sartre's analysis, because he seems to need to posit imagination as a distinct capacity in human beings, and the source of their freedom. To the skeptical reader, his distinction seems a restatement of the traditional dichotomy of mind and body, but here merely shifted into a psychological distinction among mental faculties (which have the capacity to attend to the unreal and to the real). Furthermore, as the description of his experience of the Chevalier impersonation also demonstrates, it seems clear that perceiving the real and imagining the unreal are not mutually exclusive. Whether this "proves" that imagination is a component of perception or not, it does show that the mind is capable of entertaining more than a single conception of an object simultaneously. "Multi-consciousness"[22] is a phenomenon beyond dispute in art criticism, where descriptions of experiences of art involve "analyzing out" the various simultaneous strands of those experiences.

Mary Warnock, in *Imagination,* strongly supports this objection to Sartre's theory, maintaining that Sartre ignores the fact that human beings are capable of thinking of two different things at the same time.[23] She also objects to separating the interpretative function of imagination from its image-forming function, claiming that it is difficult to clearly distinguish between perceiving the world as familiar and perceiving a portrait of a face in the canvas—both types of perception involve imagination.[24]

As Merleau-Ponty would suggest, the art object exists in its own right: it is an actual object of our consciousness (not a construct) that can be described by perceptions involving varying perspectives.[25] The very fact that the art object exists and can be perceived challenges Sartre's notion that the aesthetic object must be conceived of as wholly unreal.[26] A consequence of Sartre's assertion is that his ontology produces a drastic separation between consciousness and its object, and fails to achieve one of phenomenology's main goals—to describe consciousness as engaged in the world.[27] Sartre ultimately avoids the question of perceptual knowledge and its role in the aesthetic experience, failing to give credit to the subtlety and complexity of the aesthetic experience by not accounting for how the mind can image the aesthetic object while perceiving the real canvas and the real paint.

From Sartre's difficulties in describing "perceiving" and "imaging" in theatre, it seems that any aesthetic theory must account for both imagination and perception, not as exclusive attitudes of consciousness but as interrelated, interdependent mental activities. Though Sartre is correct when he contends that the spectator posits the object of perception as existent (actors, scenery, lighting) while positing the object of the image to be nonexistent (Hamlet, ghosts, and the castle at Elsinore), such distinctions do not satisfactorily explain the experience of drama nor provide a basis for the phenomenon of distance. That sudden jolt that Bullough describes cannot be Sartre's shift from "perceiving" to "imaging," and yet something like that (as when the treacherous fog is transformed into an otherworldly aura) does indeed occur. It is more and more clear that Sartre is pointing us toward a fundamental question with regard to the concept of distance: what role does our awareness of the objects in the theatre as "real" play in our psychological distance from the event? And how does this awareness interact with our imaginative experience of the unreal?

Though employing a different vocabulary, Sartre is similar to Bullough in making some fundamental observations. Sartre describes the "radical change" in consciousness during which "the world is negated," Bullough phrases it as the "sudden change of inward perspective." Like Bullough, when Sartre analyzes the aesthetic experience of a painting, he bases the imaginative attitude on unreality:

> [The esthetic object] will appear at the moment when consciousness, undergoing a radical change in which the world is negated, will itself become imaginative.... The Charles VIII on the canvas is necessarily the correlative of the intentional act of an imaginative consciousness. And since this Charles VIII, who is an unreality so long as he is grasped on the canvas, is precisely the object of our esthetic appreciations..., we are led to recognize that, in a picture, the esthetic object is something unreal. (p. 274)

Sartre seems to say that while perceiving the object (the canvas, brush strokes, etc.) we recognize the unreality of what it represents, which echoes Bullough's emphasis on the unreality as a consequence of the "sudden change of inward perspective." For both theorists, the basis for the viewer's experience of distance is an awareness of the unreality of the object as an aesthetic object.

Sartre also parallels Bullough when he claims that to exploit distance is to exploit the apparent contradiction that aesthetic distance permits emotional involvement. Indeed, Sartre suggests a far more satisfactory and complete theory to explain Bullough's idea than Bullough does. Bullough argues that one element of psychical distance is an emotional engagement in an object outside ourselves created by our projection of our own emotions onto that object. Sartre's view is quite consistent with this and further explains it: because theatre involves the spectator in an act of consciousness of creating an imaginary, unreal world, the spectator is on the one hand psychologically protected, the characters being the product of his will and imagination, and, on the other, the spectator is not only permitted but powerfully drawn to share the character's feelings since they are literally "owned" by the spectator—the emotions *are* his own.

However, Sartre's concept of distance significantly differs from that of Bullough in his emphasis on empathy and the direction toward which his aesthetic interests take him. Though it is clear that Sartre premises the art experience on the spectator's awareness of its unreality, he sometimes seems to want total amnesia to occur once that basis is established, pushing against one boundary of the concept of distance—at least in theory. Only when Sartre engages in a kind of polemic against nontraditional forms of theatre that over-engage the spectator by presenting literally real happenings and impose "sadistic action upon the spectator" do we get a clear signal that distance, as Bullough understands it, must be maintained. Because in the happening and the documentary play, the real is only real, "without appeal to the audience's free imagination," there is no distance to provide space for the imagination to create something from the real. This is "the point at which theatre disintegrates." It is Sartre's assertion of theoretical absolutes which causes problems for him, because this compels him to hold that what he calls "perception" and "imagination" are exclusive forms of consciousness. In contrast, Bullough's theory does not involve the annihilation of either the object or the self but an increased awareness of both. Ironically, it is in Bullough's theory that other major elements of Sartre's conception of distance fall into place: both empathy with the art object and awareness of its unreality are basic to his view, and it is precisely the double perception of the real object and the fictional object which makes the phenomenon possible.

A further implication of Sartre's dismissal of the actual as the continuing source of tension with the imaginary is that "the negation of the real" involves, on some level, a form of delusion. If this be the case, then imagination is cut loose from either grounding or guidance in the object in space and time; the image becomes free-floating and owes nothing to the perceptual object.

Perhaps the most important original contribution that Sartre makes to the understanding of distance lies in his insistence on the freedom of the imagination. He speaks of this freedom in two ways: as the source of man's freedom from the world and as a voluntary act of consciousness. There appears to be an implicit contradiction here, in that if imagination is a voluntary act then it cannot also be the source of man's freedom but a consequence of it. In any case, what one is free to do is something that one must will to do. That element of volition is implicit in both Bullough's and Brecht's concepts of distance and most salient in Sartre's. In his description of his experience of Franconay's performance he says, "I am always free to see Maurice Chevalier as an image, or as a small woman who is making faces." It is in such an extreme instance that the underlying condition of volition emerges, for in the usual experience of drama the act of will is subsumed by the decision to attend the theatre with all of the conditioning, or expectations, that such a decision entails. Sartre points out that the perception of reality is involuntary, though perhaps a learned relationship to the world, whereas "only a formal will can prevent consciousness from gliding from the level of the image to that of the perception [of reality]." That is, one must will to initiate and to sustain the imaginative act of consciousness. Indeed, if that act of consciousness is, as Sartre says, a negation of the world, that is, a conscious reconfiguration of an object as unreal, it must be willed. Therefore, if distance is understood to be this embracing of the unreal in relation to a real object then it is a voluntary act of consciousness, which would explain the sense in which Bullough feels that distance is a condition prior to the fictionality of the object.[28] Distance is not an involuntary seizure of the mind, nor an automatic (even though it may become conditioned) response to objects of a certain kind; it is an act of will. In this case then distancing techniques are not merely intensifications of our awareness of artistic conventions, or of the fictionality of the object, but reminders of our original contract with the object: that its existence as an aesthetic object rests on our complicity.

3

Heightened Awareness

Both Bullough and Sartre are primarily concerned with developing descriptions of the perceiver's psychological experience of art. For both Bullough and Sartre, distance is intrinsic to all art and is an essential characteristic of aesthetic consciousness. Theirs are formulations for general aesthetic theories. Bertolt Brecht, on the other hand, is motivated by his concern with techniques of the practical theatre: his theory of distance is for the express purpose of creating his particular kind of theatre, a "non-Aristotelian" drama. For this reason Brecht's notion is less ambitious, less complex, as it essentially probes at only one corner of the area that Bullough stakes out for the concept of distance. The narrower, focused beam of Brecht's intelligence, the long period of his concern with the question, the continual interaction of his theory with his practice, and his willingness to modify his ideas make Brecht uniquely capable of throwing a sharper light on some aspects of the distance concept.

In his 1922 *Schriften sum Theatre,* Bertolt Brecht articulates his early view of distance:

> I hope in *Baal* and *Dickicht* I've avoided one common artistic bloomer, that of trying to carry people away. Instinctively, I've kept my distance and ensured that the realization of my (poetical and philosophical) effects remains within bounds. The spectator's "splendid isolation" is left intact; it is not *sua res quae agitur;* he is not fobbed off with an invitation to feel sympathetically, to fuse with the hero and seem significant and indestructible as he watches himself in two simultaneous versions. A higher type of interest can be got from making comparisons, from whatever is different, amazing, impossible to take in as a whole.[1]

Brecht wishes to avoid "trying to carry people away," to prevent the viewer's intense emotional involvement with the hero (usually termed empathy and supposedly characteristic of western theatre) and to achieve instead a "splendid isolation" on the part of the spectator, an increased distance whereby the audience member is intellectually involved, applying critical judgments, and making valuable comparisons. For Brecht, the spectator's distance is not simply a protection from the characters'"whites of eyes," but a particular frame of mind.

Early in his career, Brecht was concerned to rid his performers and the audience members of emotion, stating that he wanted his characters to be played "coldly, classically, and objectively" because they were not meant for the spectator's mere emotional experience, but, rather, for a superior type of involvement.

> The characters are not a matter of empathy; they are there to be understood. Feelings are private and limited. Against that the reason is fairly comprehensive and to be relied on.[2]

In this early phase of his work,[3] Brecht was concerned to work on a conscious, intellectual plane instead of any subconscious or emotional level because he wanted his audience to always be thinking. In his earliest theoretical writings, Brecht stressed the use of devices and techniques that he supposed would create a rational response in the viewer as opposed to a mere emotional response, techniques that heighten the spectator's awareness of theatre by drawing attention to the use of theatrical conventions, jolting the spectator into an alert mental state.

By the 1940s, after twenty years of practical work in the theatre, it is clear from Brecht's writings that his perspective has changed; he no longer rejects emotion but has decided to use it:

> The rejection of empathy is not the result of a rejection of the emotions, nor does it lead to such. The crude aesthetic thesis that emotions can only be stimulated by means of empathy is wrong. None the less a non-aristotelian dramaturgy has to apply a cautious criticism to the emotions which it aims at and incorporates.[4]

Instead of trying to eliminate emotions, either in the performance or in the audience, Brecht argues that emotions should be used in a controlled, specific way. He no longer associates distance exclusively with intellectual involvement but instead conceives of emotion as a potentially useful element in the critical, distanced perspective he aims for in his spectators.[5]

> The representation of human behaviour from a social point of view is meant indeed to have a decisive influence on the spectator's own social behaviour. This sort of intervention is bound to release emotional effects; they are deliberate and have to be controlled. A creation that more or less renounces empathy need not by any means be an "unfeeling" creation, or one which leaves the spectator's feelings out of account. But it has to adopt a critical approach to his emotions.[6]

Brecht rejects "the crude aesthetic thesis" which had become a commonplace of the realistic theatre, that empathy is a necessary condition for stimulating emotion. This is an important distinction for Brecht, permitting him to theoretically support elements of his adopted theatrical style and yet to admit emotion-inducing techniques (or justify their use in plays he had already written). But even if empathy is to be avoided in performance, Brecht suggests that empathy can be quite useful during the rehearsal process, though he insists that it should be treated as only one method of acting.[7]

Brecht believes that traditional western, or "Aristotelian," theatre is a pacifier because empathy puts the spectator *into* the situation instead of making him or her a critical observer of it. Presumably, the spectator kept on the "outside" of the events onstage will maintain a degree of critical independence from the point of view expressed onstage, an independence that promotes "hypothetical adjustments"[8] to the drama onstage. The audience for the Epic Theatre is expected to perceive alternatives to the events: different options open to the characters, different outcomes for the various events, alternative social systems or frames of reference.

Though he continually modified his view of the role of emotions in the "alienation-effect" (also translated as estrangement and distanciation) during his career, toward the end Brecht admits that still there was not enough feeling in his productions, not enough warmth for the majority of spectators.

> Our mistakes are different from those of other theatres. Their actors are liable to display too much spurious temperament; ours often show too little of the real thing. Aiming to avoid artificial heat, we fall short in natural warmth. We make no attempt to share the emotions of the characters we portray, but these emotions must none the less be fully and movingly represented, nor must they be treated with coldness but likewise with an emotion of some force: thus, the character's despair with genuine anger on our part, or his anger with genuine despair, as the case may be. If actors in other theatres overplay the moods and outbursts of their characters that does not allow us to underplay them; nor may we overplay the story, which they are apt to underplay.[9]

In his most thoughtful and sophisticated writing, based on many years of practical theatre work, Brecht does not consider a rejection of emotion necessary for increased distance in the spectators, but rather considers it a crucial element for creating his type of theatre.

The most evident characteristics of that type of theatre which Brecht calls "Epic Theatre," are its style features, and these derive from a particular function. In his theoretical writings, Brecht stresses the use of techniques that will create a more rational response in the viewer as opposed to the more nonrational experience that he attributes to traditional theatre. He suggests a number of devices for increasing the spectator's distance by heightening awareness of theatrical conventions; some of these devices have to do with the actor, some with the stage, and some with the general orientation of the production concept.

Brecht advocates that the actors remain detached from their characters, showing the characters but not "becoming" them. He further suggests that the performers drop the fourth wall convention, directly address the audience, speak in third person, and emphasize the story as opposed to the characters themselves. Brecht often suggests that if we have the actors draw attention to themselves as performers (or as demonstrators), the audience will be more aware of the production as a theatrical event. The performer "need not pretend that the events taking place on the stage have never been rehearsed, and are now happening for the first and only time."[10] Presumably, the spectator's awareness of the event as a theatrical performance causes a more active mental participation, with the viewer realizing that he or she is not to become a part of the events but to view them as a performance,[11] perceiving them from the "outside" rather than the "inside."[12]

To avoid putting the spectator into an hypnotic "trance," the actor, Brecht believes, must himself not go into a trance, must not "identify" with the character he portrays. The actor is not to become the character but to *show* the character, which involves not the avoidance of feelings but the distinction of the actor's feelings from those of the character.[13]

> He has just to show the character, or rather he has to do more than just get into it; this does not mean that if he is playing passionate parts he must himself remain cold. It is only that his feelings must not at bottom be those of the character, so that the audience's may not at bottom be those of the character either. The audience must have complete freedom here.[14]

Neither the actor nor the spectator is to experience the same emotions as the character and should not attempt it. Although both emotionally respond, they presumably do so from a more distanced perspective, remaining on the "outside" of the characters.[15]

Brecht suggests additional ways to increase the spectator's distance, maintaining that the stage environment itself can distance the dramatic events:

> In the first production of *Die Mutter* the stage . . . was not supposed to represent any real locality; it as it were took up an attitude itself towards the incidents shown; it quoted, narrated, prepared and recalled. Its sparse indication of furniture, doors, etc. was limited to objects that had a part in the play. . . . A big canvas at the back of the stage was used for the projection of texts and pictorial documents which remained throughout the scene, so that this screen was also virtually part of the setting. Thus the stage not only used allusions to show actual rooms but also texts and pictures to show the great movement of ideas in which the events were taking place. The projections are in no way pure mechanical aids in the sense of being extras, they are no *pons asinorum;* they do not set out to help the spectator but to block him; they prevent his complete empathy, interrupt his being automatically carried away. They turn the impact into an *indirect* one.[16]

Since the stage does not use a realistic setting, the spectator is apparently not allowed to passively view the action. With pictures and texts projecting on the back wall, the audience member is presumably forced to be more conscious of the events onstage, and therefore, presumably, is more attuned to the ideas discussed rather than only the feelings of the characters.

In addition, Brecht suggests that this more distanced perspective—critically perceiving the characters and events from the "outside"—can be created by emphasizing the story rather than the characters. For Brecht, "everything hangs on the 'story'; it is the heart of the theatrical performance."[17] To highlight the story, the individual scenes are to be fitted together so that the spectator is aware of the "knots." With a noticeable separation between each scene, the audience member presumably has time to make judgments about the scene, thereby remaining independent from the events onstage.[18]

> The individual episodes have to be knotted together in such a way that the knots are easily noticed. The episodes must not succeed one another indistinguishably but must give us a chance to interpose our judgment.... The parts of the story have to be carefully set off one against the other by giving each its own structure as a play within a play. To this end it is best to agree to use titles.... The titles must include the social point, saying at the same time something about the kind of portrayal wanted, i.e. should copy the tone of a chronicle or a ballad or a newspaper or a morality.[19]

By treating each scene as a play-within-a-play, giving each a title, and setting one apart from another, Brecht again hopes to prevent a passive participation on the part of the viewer, and, instead, force the spectator to maintain an independent, critical frame of reference. By preventing a continuous, "illusionistic" representation onstage, Brecht hopes to activate a more conscious, intellectual experience which allows critical appraisal. The spectator is induced to analyze each scene specifically in terms of its own structure and meaning and in relation to its title.

Besides emphasizing the story as a means for increasing distance, Brecht employs "historicization" to cause the spectator to view events within a temporally remote socio-economic reality. One way in which Brecht seeks to provoke such awareness in the spectator is by emphasizing the "social impulses" of the period:

> If we ensure that our characters on the stage are moved by social impulses and that these differ according to the period, then we make it harder for the spectator to identify himself with them. He cannot simply feel: that's how I would act, but at most can say: if I had lived under those circumstances. And if we play works dealing with our own time as though they were historical, then perhaps the circumstances under which he himself acts will strike him as equally odd; and this is where the critical attitude begins.[20]

Through the historicization device, playing the actions, ideas, feelings, and characters "within the particular historical field of human relations" in which they take place,[21] Brecht intends to cause the viewer to see the context in which the characters live in a critical perspective. An emphasis on the social and economic context presumably increases distance by widening the spectator's perspective, heightening the viewer's awareness of the socio-economic system onstage as being but one system among other possible systems. Historicization is for Brecht a specific distancing device that has special value for throwing a socio-economic system into relief. Encouraged to make comparisons between the character's behavior and his possible options in the social and historical context, the spectator is placed in a position to make judgments.[22]

It is important for Brecht to show that man is alterable, conditioned by an alterable social environment. He wishes to portray "man himself as dependent on certain political and economic factors and at the same time as capable of altering them."[23] For Brecht, another way to demonstrate the alterability of human beings is by showing the causal relationships of actions,[24] how a particular action is related to a number of events. In Brecht's view, that human beings are changeable and that there exists a causal relation between events can both be demonstrated by a particular method:

> The attitude which [the actor] adopts is a socially critical one. In his exposition of the incidents and in his characterization of the person he tries to bring out of those features which come within society's sphere. In this way his performance becomes a discussion about social conditions according to what class he belongs to.
>   The object of the A-effect is to alienate the social gest underlying every incident. By social gest is meant the mimetic and gestural expression of the social relationships prevailing between people of a given period.[25]

In Brecht's view, the actor is to explicitly demonstrate the ways in which the character is affected by society—its social classes, its economic system, and its political form.

Although Brecht's theory of distance is firmly entrenched in his political and social views of the world, his distancing techniques are, for the most part, designed to emphasize the difference between theatrical performances and real-life occurrences. By advocating that the theatre created only "partial illusions"—highlighting our recognition that we are witnessing a fiction— Brecht wants to stress that ordinary events when viewed from a surprising perspective can alter our perception of life. By taking scenes that have some similarity to real-world phenomena and presenting them in a self-consciously theatrical way (that is, the recognizable made distant, a reformulation of the romantic theory of the familiar made strange), Brecht wants to suggest the contingency of phenomena and to awaken the spectator's critical examination of their causes: if the event should be altered and could be altered, then the spectator will have learned to take a more active stance toward similar phenomena and their causes in his or her own world. By forcing the audience to take a more critical attitude, Brecht hopes to actually make theatre more "geared into reality,"[26] that is, make theatre have real-world implications.

For Brecht, the artist's purpose is to create the element of surprise in the spectator's perceptual experience:

The artist's object is to appear strange and even surprising to the audience. He achieves this by looking strangely at himself and his work. As a result everything put forward by him has a touch of the amazing. Everyday things are thereby raised above the level of the obvious and automatic.[27]

By concentrating on the remarkable, the alienation technique is to portray human social incidents as striking, as something requiring explanation.[28] For Brecht, "a representation that alienates is one which allows us to recognize its subject, but at the same time makes it seem unfamiliar." Alienation techniques are "designed to free socially-conditioned phenomena from that stamp of familiarity which protects them against our grasp today."[29] For Brecht, the artist's central aim is to jolt the passively viewing spectator into a more conscious, alert mental state by focusing on the unusual, by forcing the viewer to see characters and events in a new way, to perceive them within a new context. In this way the characters' actions will be perceived not as the ordinary turn of events, or as inevitable, but will be looked at with a fresh view, with an attempt to understand why the character, being the type of person he or she is, does these particular actions.

It has been recognized that Brecht's concept of alienation is quite similar to Victor Shklovsky's concept of "defamiliarization"—to make strange. Shklovsky is concerned with those literary devices that impede perception, techniques that force an awareness on the reader, causing him or her to notice details, thereby viewing the object in a fresh new way.

Art exists that one may recover the sensation of life; it exists to make one feel things, to make the stone *stony*. The purpose of art is to impart the sensation of things as they are perceived and not as they are known. The technique of art is to make objects "unfamiliar," to make forms difficult, to increase the difficulty and length of perception because the process of perception is an aesthetic end in itself and must be prolonged.[30]

For Shklovsky, the device itself is "laid bare" to be noticed by the reader.[31]

Like Shklovsky, Brecht thinks of the alienation-effect as the means by which to jolt the spectators out of their habitual response, causing them to consciously attend to the forms of theatre and the habits of thought. Brecht wants to revolutionize the way spectators perceive events on the stage, as well as to radicalize the way they perceive reality.[32] To alter the spectator's mode of perceiving, Brecht uses techniques such as surprising juxtaposition that he thinks will create a conscious response in the perceiver.

Although their theories are very similar in important ways, Brecht's theory of alienation is directed exclusively toward a social significance involving Marxist ideology, whereas Shklovsky's notion of "making strange" concerns the nature of art itself rather than any particular significance a work may have. Shklovsky describes "making strange" in terms of devices that make the reader more aware of his or her act of perception. Although Brecht does want the spectators to be aware of their act of perception, he wants such awareness to be within the "larger picture"—perceiving the events onstage within the context of the real world. Whereas, some critics argue, Shklovsky's "defamiliarization" is a purely aesthetic concept because Shklovsky primarily describes art as refreshing perception, Brecht's concern goes beyond aesthetics: his concept of alienation has a social aim—to strike at the perceptions the spectator has of himself, to shock people out of a passive, fatalistic acceptance of the events.[33] To both shock perceptions and create new contexts within which to view such perceptions, are crucial elements in Brecht's view of increased distance.

For Brecht, then, increased distance involves a number of elements, distinguishable from one another yet closely related as functions within Brecht's political aesthetic. In his view, increased distance is an increased awareness of the fictionality of the work and an intellectual understanding of its structure and meaning. This produces a dislocation of associations, forcing the viewer to perceive events within a new context; it creates a larger perspective, causing the spectator to view the characters and events from the "outside," thereby applying critical judgment; and it encourages the development of an historical perspective toward one's own time, demonstrating to the audience that events must be viewed within a particular "historical field."

Most of Brecht's alienation techniques are attempts to emphasize the fictionality of the theatrical event, creating what he refers to in his writings as a "partial illusion." According to Brecht, "the illusion created in the theatre must be a partial one, in order that it may always be viewed as an illusion. Reality, however complete, has to be altered by being turned into art, so that it can be seen to be alterable and be treated as such."[34]

It is Brecht's assumption that without his strenuous efforts the spectator would be mesmerized in the theatre, totally deluded into a transference dream-state. What Brecht wants instead is a critical perspective on the part of the spectator, one he thinks can be achieved by creating "partial illusions." By "partial illusion" Brecht seems to refer to a need for the image to be at once recognizable and distanced, which seems essentially identical to Coleridge's definition of illusion or "poetic faith."[35] Brecht seems to be maintaining that the "reality, however complete," becomes art when it is perceived as fiction (that is, when it is "recognized as an illusion"). He apparently means two things by his word "illusion": fiction and delusion. Therefore what he means by "partial illusion" is the awareness of fiction (that is, the delusion removed). In this sense Brecht is merely asking that the theatre be art.

This rather basic assumption colors the major tenets of Brecht's theory of distance: his distancing techniques are primarily devices to exaggerate what is inherent in art in order that art will be effective propaganda. Brecht wants the spectator to view theatrical performances not as simple reality—neither as the spectator's own life nor more generally as "the way things are"—but as fiction; in this way true art will be truly propagandistic (and only true art will serve this function) because the spectator will see that the character's fate is determined only by his alterable frame of reference. Brecht believes that "the theatre must acquire . . . the same fascinating reality as a sporting arena during a boxing match. The best thing is to show the machinery, the ropes and the flies."[36] He wants to gear the spectators to experience on a conscious plane, so that they are perceiving and thinking about events onstage, yet simultaneously are aware that their perceptions and thoughts are occurring in a theatre, that is, in terms of a fictional and conditional *model* of reality.

But the question arises, will an increased awareness of the mechanics of the theatre, its conventions and devices, necessarily create a critical attitude? In Elizabethan drama, the performers directly address the audience with soliloquies and asides, yet still spectators may be empathically involved. When the actor playing Hamlet delivers a soliloquy to the audience, it seems unlikely that the spectators are so conscious of the performance that they have no empathic response to the character. Or, in *Henry V*, when the Chorus points out that the events take place within "this wooden o," the purpose—and certainly the effect—is not to make the spectator more skeptical, but less.

Obviously, then, the conventions themselves do not increase awareness when they are *accepted*. As Susan Sontag points out, even the most radical of techniques become accepted conventions.

> The theory of art as assault on the audience . . . is understandable, and precious. Still, one must not neglect to question it, particularly in the theatre. For it can become as much a convention as anything else; and end, like all theatrical conventions, by reinforcing the deadness of the audience.[37]

All theatre is conventional—existing on covenants between stage and auditorium—precisely to ally skepticism, to permit the suspension of disbelief, rather than to require either belief or disbelief. This is why calling attention to the limitations of the stage in the prologue to *Henry V* does not intensify our skepticism: it reinforces the covenant. The question that remains, then, is whether increased awareness of the "fictionality" of the work (by whatever means that awareness is actually increased) necessarily produces a "critical" response, or if it does, whether the response necessarily excludes all other responses (such as an empathic one).

In addition, it is not at all self-evident that Brecht's techniques always serve Brecht's theories. Brecht insists that with the alienation technique of juxtaposition, the effect is produced because various theatrical elements are not working together to create one unified scene. The devices each work "independently," creating almost a visual and aural collage. The audience response, then, is supposedly one of intellectual involvement, as the spectator attempts to understand the thematic connections between the disparate theatrical elements.

It is not at all clear, however, that a juxtaposition of various stimuli necessarily creates an independent, critical response in the spectator. If "the most heterogeneous ideas [images] are yoked by violence together," as Dr. Johnson says of the Metaphysical Poets,[38] it may be that the illusion of intellectuality does not adequately, nor—at the deepest levels—accurately, describe the process. The method creates metaphors, not syllogisms. What seems to be occurring is the astonishment of the intellect by elements which have no logical nor natural coherence but which "make sense" metaphorically: cognitive dissonance is resolved by noncognitive consonance. Brecht's "metaphysical poetry" of the theatre stimulates, provokes, involves the spectator's mental participation—but is neither more nor less rational than any other effective poetry.

By employing a number of devices that presumably work independently, Brecht is suggesting that the viewer is forced consciously to attend the stimuli onstage from a critical perspective. But does an awareness of photographic images projected on a screen above the stage, for example, necessarily exclude an emphatic involvement with the characters on the stage, and necessarily create a critical perspective? It seems unlikely that if the projected images consist of traumatic scenes of war, and the major characters in the play are suffering from the disasters of war, the viewer will be so intellectually conscious of the unusual theatre techniques as to be unable to empathically respond to the performers as characters.

Brecht's position that the actor's emotion be portrayed "independently" of the character's emotions poses another difficulty with his theory.

> We make no attempt to share the emotions of the characters we portray, but these emotions must none the less be fully and movingly represented.[39]

If the emotions of characters must be fully and movingly represented, who is "moved"? It is clear that Brecht is referring to the emotions of the characters, the actors, and the audience, and while it is true that each may be a distinct emotion, it is also clear that the juxtaposition of the character's emotion against the actor's must induce the spectator's. However, this juxtaposition does not require a critical response (nor does it produce a new kind of "non-Aristotelian" theatre). When a character such as Richard III manipulates another character by "playing a role," the pretended emotion is juxtaposed against the "real" one and the spectator's sense of irony and skepticism is aroused on the same principle of juxtaposition but in totally traditional terms. The same technique is employed by Canio in *I Pagliacci*[40] who pretends to laugh while he is in agony, disarming the spectator's skepticism and unloosing a flood of tears. When the Restoration actor turns to the audience with an aside expressing a very different attitude from that of his character, the affect is a familiar conspiracy of laughter. It is not, as Brecht avers, the technique alone which creates alienation: the technique merely surprises the spectator into recognizing the social criticism if it is there.

The question is whether Brecht's techniques, conventions, and stylistic devices demand critical thinking at all, whether they create in the viewer a critical independence of the characters onstage. Rather than merely techniques it becomes a matter of the fusion of techniques and *content:* a political consciousness, on the simplest level, is raised by the subject matter, to which attention is drawn by the distancing devices. The ideas presented through the dramatic fiction, highlighted by the artistic devices employed, are the means through which political views are altered.

Like Brecht, Bullough talks about a "wider consciousness," whereby the viewer suddenly sees beyond the merely immediate, as in the example of the fog, and obtains a larger frame of reference, as in the case of art. It may be that this larger perspective, which Bullough contends is characteristic of all art, becomes political when it results from a particular content that encourages such a point of view. The techniques are informed by a context which becomes potent by those techniques. *Mother Courage* may make us indignant about our social system of competitive survival not only because it is presented in the Epic Theatre style but because the Thirty Years' War is made a powerful metaphor through that style.

In the case of a play such as *Oedipus,* a production may use some of the same theatrical devices and conventions (e.g., direct address, song) as a production of *Mother Courage,* but the larger perspective induced at the end of the play will not necessarily be political because of those techniques. *Oedipus,* through its subject matter and its overall dramatic structure, creates, as Brecht would want, a "larger perspective" at the end in that the entire play is seen in a new light: past events in the play "make sense" within the context of our new understanding of the action at the end of the play. The larger perspective, comprehension of the action in light of its resolution, includes a perception of the action in relation to the real world—that is, its metaphorical significance. Just as Brecht would hope for, a real-world context is provided for the play, but in this case the "gearing into reality" concerns not political but cosmic issues.

Though Brecht wants plays such as *Mother Courage* to prevent an empathic involvement, he may be pushing his theory further than it can go. After reading press notices and talking with audience members, Brecht realized that the audience responded to "the characters' more emotional utterances" while forgetting the rest of the play.[41] In order to emphasize that Mother Courage is determined to carry on her business activity no matter what, and to preclude identification with her, after the Munich production of 1950, Brecht added a new last line to Mother Courage's final speech: "I must get back into business."[42] Brecht continued to complain that many actresses played Mother

Courage as a tragedy rather than stressing her callous businesslike attitude in the final scene. Instead of tragic empathy, Brecht wants the audience to recognize that Mother Courage has learnt nothing from her experiences.[43]

Brecht employs alienation techniques as a means for *exceeding* aesthetic distance. By increasing the spectator's awareness of the theatre as theatre, Brecht wishes to decrease the effects of empathy and, especially, to force the spectator to confront his world with the principles he has been observing in the play. Brecht uses direct address and other such devices to control the spectator's awareness of the external resonances of the play as it progresses: it is as if the play were a painted curtain between the spectator and the real world, a curtain which Brecht parts at calculated moments. In this respect Sartre does not so much disagree with Brecht about the consequences of the use of devices such as direct address so much as he does about the desirability of those consequences. A destruction of empathy is not what Sartre finds most valuable in the art experience. Whereas Brecht seeks an attenuation or disruption of empathy, a critical independence, and a generally high level of awareness of theatre as theatre, Sartre prefers an intense identification with a minimum awareness of the fictionality of the theatre event (since perception can annihilate imaging).

Though Bullough implies that distance has to do with an awareness of fiction, an appreciation of its "*art*-character," he explicitly rejects fictionality as a cause, claiming it to be an effect of distance. Brecht, however, sees an increased awareness of fiction as an essential ingredient for a more distanced perspective. His alienation techniques are primarily devices to highlight the difference between real-life and theatrical productions, whereby the spectator is continually made aware that he or she is in a theatre.

Similar to Brecht's "alienation," Bullough often mentions a "sudden change of inward perspective," both in terms of describing an aesthetic response to the fog, and when analyzing the aesthetic experience in the theatre. For Bullough, this sudden change in perspective refers to a perception of unreality that initiates a new way of seeing the object—that is, a new context or frame of reference for it. This jolting of perception is quite similar to Brecht's specific concept of alienation as a dislocation of associations. Whereas Bullough analyzes this "larger perspective" more generally, describing this change of attitude as the adoption of an aesthetic attitude, Brecht pushes the notion to a socio-political level of explanation, referring to the establishment of a political perspective, experiencing the object beyond itself within the context of the real world. Concerned with the effects of his Epic Theatre, Brecht stresses that ordinary events when viewed from a surprising perspective can alter our perception of life. Developing an aesthetic theory, Bullough maintains that our altered perception of life (as in the example of the fog) results in an aesthetic experience.

For Bullough, distance allows the perceiver to view the work "objectively," creating a "personal" but "filtered" relation to the work, preventing a *direct* emotional involvement. Emotions are experienced pseudo-vicariously, without a personal objective; one's own feelings are attributed to the object outside of the self. Like Bullough, Brecht also maintains that distance increases "objectivity." But whereas Bullough sees "objectivity" as a lack of a personal objective, Brecht is after a larger socio-economic perspective to which the spectator *can* relate him or herself. Objectivity for Brecht's Epic Theatre is not the projection of the spectator's emotions into fictional characters, as Bullough describes, but rather more like that of science, it is a condition in which the spectator may critically judge the behavior of the characters. Brecht most specifically objects to empathy, the emotional projection into the characters (which is central to Bullough's theory), and maintains that distance blocks such emotional investment. But as Eric Bentley points out, in Brecht's Epic Theatre illusion and suspense are not eliminated but merely de-emphasized: "[Brecht] does not eliminate stage-illusion and suspense: he only reduces their importance. Sympathy and identification with the characters are not eliminated; they are counterpoised by deliberate distancing."[44] Although Brecht is theoretically opposed to empathy, and would object to Bullough's notion of an investment of emotion in the fictional characters, his own plays do not eliminate such empathic responses.

When Bullough discusses Greek tragedy, he claims that its temporal remoteness removes the dangers of a personal reaction to the work (here asserting the more Kantian notion of "disinterestedness"), allowing us a greater appreciation of its "*art*-character." Brecht makes a parallel argument to Bullough's but arrives at an opposite conclusion. Brecht maintains that this temporal remoteness permits the spectator to make rational assessments in terms of his own self-interest—how the work relates to his own life and the real world. Whereas for Bullough, distance blocks the concrete, practical appeal of the object, for Brecht, increased distance induces a "practical attitude," causing the viewer to perceive the work in light of the necessities of the concrete world.

For these reasons, Bullough calls for the "least amount of distance without its disappearance," seeming to mean the least amount of awareness of the work as artifice that can still prevent an excess of empathic involvement. Brecht, on the other hand, advocates the greatest increase of distance that still does not prevent the pleasures of entertainment and story—that is, of art. For Brecht, theatre should increase the spectator's awareness of fictionality in order to induce a self-interested involvement, permitting a critical appraisal of the object in terms of its relevance to his or her real world.

Brecht, as a playwright, was deliberately and consciously beating against the limits of extreme distancing in order to create social understanding, in contrast to Bullough, whose purpose in his essay was to describe a general aesthetic principle.

As noted at the beginning of this chapter, in the evolution of Brecht's aesthetic his concept of distance, and of what degree of dispassion is desirable or possible, altered greatly. By the end of his life he had not only begun to acknowledge in his writings the importance of emotional responses by the spectator (and to remonstrate with his actors to employ emotion), he seems also to have implicitly recognized the functional value of empathic responses for achieving his goals. He had tested the limits of extreme distancing and, instead of following it beyond art and theatre, by the time of the writing of "A Short Organum," he explicitly pulled back from that boundary. He wants, as he writes in "A Short Organum," a "theatre as a place of entertainment, as is proper in an aesthetic discussion."[45] As Bullough suggests, there is a limit only within which the intensification of distance serves art. But there is no doubt that Brecht demonstrates in his work that the limits exceed anything that Bullough contemplated.

4

Psychological Protection from Fiction

For Jean-Paul Sartre , aesthetic distance essentially deals with the unreal: the theatre production reveals the nonexistent image (of the unreal) through the real (actors, scenery, etc.). Sartre claims that by trying to present "reality" to the spectators, contemporary theatre artists undermine theatre's special relation of real to unreal, thereby minimizing distance, confusing the audience, and creating a muddled effect. The attempt to reduce the distinction between the "real" and the "unreal" is a crucial characteristic of the theories of both Jerzy Grotowski and Antonin Artaud, both of whom are theatre practitioners wanting to eliminate the division between actors and audience and to do away with the separation of theatre from life. As with Brecht, Artaud's and Grotowski's theories are determined by their immediate concerns with the practical theatre.

When asked why his actors never use laughter or humor to acquire some distance from what they are doing, Jerzy Grotowski responded:

> For us, there is something of fun here, but what is at the foundation, at the core, is very serious indeed. This was not our original idea, but isn't what regards life (how to live) very serious in some way? On the other hand, could the introduction of elements of humor or laughter introduce distance? Possibly. But is this a duty? Don't we treat too many things in life with distance? Are there no such matters... which one should tackle directly, without distancing?...If at any time big laughter, or fun, become the obvious and natural thing to do for us, we will admit them, give them vent, for if one feels the need for laughter, or fun, one has to give way to it. If one doesn't, one mustn't. But we will not do it in order to bring in distance. We will do it to give way to the need for the big laughter, absolutely without distance.[1]

Grotowski wants to do away with the emotional withdrawal and the psychological protection characteristic of western theatre because he wants theatre to be "very serious indeed," attacking "essential and fundamental" matters "directly, without distancing." Grotowski is saying that life is *real* and that he is treating its reality; to distance it would suggest unreality.

This earnestness produces for both Growtowski and Artaud an aesthetic apparently founded on the elimination of distance, on a direct assault on the psyches of the spectators. For them, theatre should be comparable to a deeply felt religious event, a ritual of sorts. Grotowski likens the performance of the actor to a religious sacrifice. The actor completely strips himself (that is, emotionally, psychologically, spiritually) to totally reveal his inner self to the audience, to make "a total gift of himself" to the spectators. For Grotowski, "this is a technique of the 'trance' and of the integration of all the actor's psychic and bodily powers which emerge from the most intimate layers of his being and his instinct, springing forth in a sort of 'translumination.'"[2] The actor's sacrificial vulnerability to the audience is referred to by Grotowski as a "secular holiness."

> The actor's wretchedness can be transformed into a kind of..."secular holiness." If the actor, by setting himself a challenge publicly challenges others, and through excess, profanation and outrageous sacrilege reveals himself by casting off his everyday mask, he makes it possible for the spectator to undertake a similar process of self-penetration. If he does not exhibit his body, but annihilates it, burns it, frees it from every resistance to any psychic impulse, then he does not sell his body but sacrifices it. He repeats the atonement; he is close to holiness.[3]

Through the actor's self-sacrifice, theatre can presumably achieve a therapeutic function by establishing a fulfilled encounter between actor and spectator, a "total act" which "epitomizes the actor's deepest calling."[4]

In a remarkably similar fashion,[5] both in terms of language and central premises, Artaud calls for a ritualistic theatre that will thrust theatre back into real life.[6] Artaud does not want the spectator to perceive a division between life and theatre:

> There must be no let up, no vacuum in the audience's mind or sensitivity. That is to say there will be no distinct divisions, no gap between life and theatre.[7]

Whereas Christian Metz characterizes the film as the "vacuum, which dreams readily fill," meaning that the medium has an inherent minimum of distance that allows for the spectator's projections into the film, Artaud (who was a film actor) wants "no vacuum" in the mind of the theatre spectator, no part of the psyche not filled with sensation—and therefore no part of it reserved to observe itself.

Artaud claims that theatre must break away from its contemporary psychologizing and, instead, seek to express "secret truths, to bring out in active gestures those elements of truth hidden under forms in their encounters with Becoming," by restoring theatre to a religious, metaphysical position (p. 51), to communicate with the audience on an inner level (pp. 70-71). Artaud wishes theatre to have a significant impact by restoring to it a sense of necessity, as felt in ritual, and as suggested by his metaphor of the plague:

For if theatre is like the plague, this is not just because it acts on large groups and disturbs them in one and the same way. There is both something victorious and vengeful in theatre just as in the plague, for we clearly feel that spontaneous fire the plague lights as it passes by nothing but gigantic liquidation. (p. 18)...

... Like the plague, theatre is a crisis resolved either by death or cure. The plague is a superior disease because it is an absolute crisis after which there is nothing left except death or drastic purification. In the same way, theatre is a disease because it is a final balance that cannot be obtained without destruction. It urges the mind on to delirium which intensifies its energy. (p. 22)

For Artaud, this sense of necessity in theatre should seem "victorious and vengeful," being "resolved either by death or cure," not "without destruction." Artaud here suggests that, like the plague, theatre should affect its participants "directly," without psychological removal from the event, and without psychological protection from the "absolute crisis" manifest in the intensity of the spectacle.

The major technique to abolish psychological distance, for both Artaud and Grotwoski, is to do away with the physical distance between actor and audience, or to significantly alter it.

Artaud wants to affect every aspect of the spectator's sensibility with a "revolving show" (p. 66), doing away with the stage and auditorium and replacing them with direct contact between the audience and the show: "the audience is seated in the centre of action, is encircled and furrowed by it" (p. 74). By extending "visual and oral outbursts over the whole mass of spectators" (p. 66), to all corners of the auditorium, Artaud wants to create a pervasive sense of urgency, thereby presumably preventing the audience from assuming the role of mere spectators. In addition, by emphasizing the tactile and the nonvisual, Artaud wants the spectator to move beyond merely seeing the event to actually experiencing it sensually and aurally, thereby feeling the immediate impact of the spectacle. Artaud suggests that his Theatre of Cruelty bombard the spectator with "physical images," sounds, pictures, movement, dance, mime, music, lights, creating "violent physical images," "a bloodshed of images, a bloody spurt of images" that will "pulverise, mesmerize the audience's sensibilities" (pp. 62-63). With the physical images speaking directly to the mind,[8] the spectator will be "antagonized by the internal dynamic of the spectacle," and the dichotomy between subject and object will be destroyed as the theatre creates a total identification in the audience as they "identify with the show breath by breath and beat by beat" (p. 95).

What seems to be implicit in Artaud's concept of theatre is made explicit by Grotowski: that the challenge of the photographic media must be met by theatre on its own ground, that theatre must radically exploit its special virtue of presentness.

There is only one element of which film and television cannot rob the theatre: the closeness of the living organism. Because of this, each challenge from the actor, each of his magical acts (which the audience is incapable of reproducing) becomes something great, something extraordinary, something close to ecstacy. It is therefore necessary to abolish the distance between actor and audience by eliminating the stage, removing all frontiers. Let the most drastic scenes happen face to face with the spectator so that he is within arm's reach of the actor, can feel his breathing and smell the perspiration.[9]

Like Artaud, Grotowski wants to bombard the spectator sensually in order to get at inner truths. Through "outrageous excess," Grotowski wants the audience to return to "a concrete mythical situation, an experience of common human truth."[10] By shocking the audience, the actors can presumably help the spectators remove their outer masks of artificialities.[11]

In this struggle with one's own truth, this effort to peel off the life-mask, the theatre, with its full-fleshed perceptivity, has always seemed to me a place of provocation. It is capable of challenging itself and its audience by violating accepted stereotypes of vision, feeling, and judgment—more jarring because it is imaged in the human organism's breath, body, and inner impulses.[12]

Due to its physicality, its direct contact with other human beings, theatre, in Grotowski's view, can be the ultimate "place of provocation" which challenges the audience's stereotypical vision of the world, "jarring" them into perceiving the world and their "own truth" in a new way. Both Artaud and Grotowski want theatre to attain the unreserved seriousness of ritual, the spiritual and metaphysical power of religious transformation.

Attempting to place such views in a larger perspective, Richard Schechner makes a distinction between ritual drama, that is, the "social drama" of tribal or community religious theatre, and "aesthetic drama," the evolved theatre of western secular civilization, on the basis of the relation of spectator and actor.

Aesthetic drama works a transformation on the audience who is separate from the performers. This separation is a chief evidence of the existence of aesthetic drama. In social [ritual] drama all present are participants, though some are more decisively involved than others. In aesthetic drama everyone in the theatre is a participant in the *performance* while only those playing roles in the drama are participants in the dramatic event nested within the performance event.... The function of aesthetic drama is to do for the consciousness of the audience what social drama does for its participants: to provide a place for, and a means of, transformation. Rituals carry participants across limits transforming them into different persons.[13]

Whereas rituals mystically transform those who are actual participants in them (e.g., freeing them from the evil powers), Schechner argues that aesthetic drama works to affect a transformation in the nonparticipating spectator's consciousness. Because the spectator is separated from the performance in aesthetic drama, has both physical and psychological distance from the event, the viewer is affected by the performance, but not on the same level as ritual. When aesthetic distance is present, the consciousness of the viewer may be affected, but apparently not to the extent of total transformation (so as to produce a religious conversion, for instance).

Though Schechner makes his point in terms of participation versus witnessing, his more fundamental distinction seems essentially between belief (ritual) and suspension of disbelief (aesthetic drama). Ritual does not exist in a vacuum but requires a social fabric and a deeply felt belief system to have effect.

Roger Copeland argues that because Artaud's theories advocate a "return to ritual" they are premised on the antithesis of aesthetic distance.

> Artaud's efforts to restore a sense of necessity to the theatre (and to life) is ultimately an attack on the very concept of "aesthetic distance" (which Kant called "disinterested interest"). Susan Sontag has written that "art is seduction, not rape (and) art cannot seduce without the complicity of the experiencing subject." But it is precisely that freedom (ultimately, the freedom to say "no") that Artaud would deny the spectator in the name of necessity. "This idea of a disinterested art," he writes, "is a decadent idea."... Artaud's project consists of nothing less than an all-out assault on the very idea of theatre, a challenge to the theatrical nature of modern consciousness.... One cannot return to ritual without first destroying the very concept of the theatre as a *theatron* or seeing place.[14]

Copeland confronts a fundamental issue in Artaud's theory, but in doing so he blurs and somewhat confuses distinct concepts. Kant uses the term "disinterestedness" to refer to the contemplation of an object that involves "disinterested and *free* satisfaction."[15] Copeland shifts the meaning when he refers to Kant's concept as "disinterested interest" (paralleling Kant's "purposeful purposelessness"), thereby reflecting his own awareness of post-Kantian thinking which has emphasized a more personal involvement in the art work. Kant, however, explicitly rules out the element of "interest" when explaining "disinterestedness":

> A judgement upon an object of our delight may be wholly *disinterested*, but withal very *interesting*, i.e. it relies on no interest, but it produces one. Of this kind are all pure moral judgements. But, of themselves, judgements of taste do not set up any interest whatsoever. Only in society is it *interesting* to have taste.[16]

In addition, Copeland confounds the concepts of distance and disinterestedness with his parenthetical qualifier: "the very concept of 'aesthetic distance' (which Kant called 'disinterested interest')." Bullough describes distance as a psychological state in which one's personal interest is "encapsulated" and projected onto a fictitious object. By this means Bullough is able to explain how a spectator's very real interest, however passionate, may be conceived in *retrospect* as a kind of intense yet disinterested attention.

But does Artaud's theory, as Copeland suggests, require the condition of belief that is essential to ritual? Though Artaud wants theatre to be viewed as a "ceremony" that has significant implications for life in the world, and to have even greater impact than real-life events, his discussion clearly implies that he premises everything he says on a distinction between theatre and reality:

> We believe there are living powers in what is called poetry, and that a picture of a crime presented in the right stage conditions is something infinitely more dangerous to the mind than if the same crime were committed in life.
> We want to make theatre a believable reality inflicting this kind of tangible laceration.... In the same way as our dreams react on us and reality reacts on our dreams; so we believe ourselves able to associate mental pictures with dreams, effective in so far as they are projected with the required violence. And the audience will believe in the illusion of theatre on the condition they really take it for a dream, not for a servile imitation of reality. On condition it releases the magic freedom of daydreams, only recognisable when imprinted with terror and cruelty. (p. 65)

Though he does not analyze it, nor is he perhaps even aware of it, it seems clear that Artaud's concept of illusion[17] requires that the spectator hold a certain distance from the work, even an awareness of fiction: a stage crime is *more* dangerous than a real one, illusion is accepted on condition that it not be a pretended reality. Contrary to Copeland's analysis, even this self-described "hypnotic" theory of drama is posited on a concept of distance. Artaud's first premise is that the "illusion of theatre" is conditioned on our knowing that it *is* theatre that we are going to—which he describes as a place of waking dreams—and not to a surrogate reality that merely reflects a weakened image of ourselves back on ourselves.

Artaud wants his theatre to be taken seriously, not as amusement nor mere entertainment but as a place for profoundly significant events and therefore for an equally profound effect on the spectator, transforming him or her in actual life. All great art seems to aspire to effect such a transformation in its viewers— certainly art manifestos usually have such ambitions. Although Artaud speaks of his ambitions in terms similar to those used by Schechner in his description of ritual, and, indeed, Artaud employs religious language, it is as serious a misunderstanding of him to take this metaphorical usage literally as it would be to take literally his "plague" metaphor.[18] Though theatre is to be "serious,"it is, for Artaud, a "serious game":

> With [each] performance we put on we are playing a serious game, that the whole point of our effort resides in this quality of seriousness. It is not to the minds or the senses of the spectators that we address ourselves but to their whole existence. Their existence and ours. We stake our own lives on the spectacle that unfolds on the stage.... The spectator who comes to our theatre knows that he is to undergo a real operation in which not only his mind but his sense and his flesh are at stake. Henceforth he will go to the theatre the way he goes to the surgeon or the dentist. In the same state of mind—knowing, of course, that he will not die, but that it is a serious thing, and that he will not come out of it unscathed. If we were not convinced that we would reach him as deeply as possible, we would consider ourselves inadequate to our most absolute duty. He must be totally convinced that we are capable of making him scream.[19]

For those who play the game, theatre can be a kind of surgery on the mind—just that serious—and yet only the game-condition that the spectator knows "that he will not die" permits so serious an operation to occur. Artaud's mixed metaphor, in which the theatre is at once a game and a surgical amphitheatre, is an attempt to express the qualifying conditions: that is, it seems, the theatre is a protected environment in which one can permit oneself to be most vulnerable because he is most safe, and therefore can expose himself to one kind of spiritual and psychological reality most completely because he is protected from physical reality. A game has rule-boundaries only within which its reality operates; and, while operations of a different kind, with a different reality, take place in a surgical amphitheatre, it is a special place, a place distinguishable from all others.

With a metaphor similar to that of Artaud, Grotowski refers to the role of the actor as a "surgeon's scalpel."

> The decisive factor in this process is the actor's technique of psychic penetration. He must learn to use his role as if it were a surgeon's scalpel, to dissect himself. It is not a question of portraying himself under certain given circumstances, or of "living" a part; nor does it entail the distant sort of acting common to epic theatre and based on cold calculation. The important thing is to use the role as a trampoline, an instrument with which to study what is hidden behind our everyday mask—the innermost core of our personality—in order to sacrifice it, expose it.
>
> This is an excess not only for the actor but also for the audience. The spectator understands, consciously or unconsciously, that such an act is an invitation to him to do the same thing, and this often arouses opposition or indignation, because our daily efforts are intended to hide the truth about ourselves not only from the world, but also from ourselves. We try to escape the truth about ourselves, whereas here we are invited to stop and take a closer look.[20]

Grotowski, like Artaud, is suggesting that the actor affect the spectator directly, touching the inner depths of the viewer's psyche in order that both the actor and spectator can strip themselves of their defenses, their "everyday mask," to get to the person underneath. And yet, even this attempt at direct confrontation and self-revelation is premised on distance: the spectator is aware, "consciously or unconsciously," that the actor's performance is separate from him or her, and that it is an "invitation." Implied in the voluntary nature of the event is that the spectator has the choice to accept the performance and respond to it, or to reject it and choose not to engage in self-penetration. The very fact that Grotowski mentions that "opposition or indignation" often occurs in the audience points to the freedom of the audience members to respond in a variety of ways, resulting from the fact that the event is, and *must* be, on the level of an "invitation." There is not the necessity of either ritual or a real-life event in the performance: the viewer is aware that this is an actor before him, and the spectator's response is voluntary.

It is interesting that Grotowski, like Brecht, invites the spectator to identify with the *actor* rather than with the character, though he dismisses epic theatre as "coldly calculating." For Brecht it is the actor's distance and skeptical attitude which the spectator shares; for Grotowski, it is the actor's agony of total self-exposure which is shared.

Though the sensual assault on the spectator is thought by Artaud and Grotowski to be a means of directly attacking the audience and thereby destroying distance, some theorists maintain that "assault" techniques may actually increase distance by initially creating an intense emotional response (the very shock that Artaud and Grotowski desire), followed by a critical reflection on that response. Peter Brook explains how the "happening effect" is similar to the "alienation effect" in that both attempt to jolt the audience.

> The alienation effect and the happening effect are similar and opposite—the happening shock is there to smash through all the barriers set up by our reason, alienation is to shock us into bringing the best of our reason into play.[21]

Brook goes on to explain that the "happening effect" occurs

> the moment when the illogical breaks through our everyday understanding to make us open our eyes more widely. The whole play has established questions and references: the moment of surprise is a jolt to the kaleidoscope, and what we see in the playhouse we can retain and relate to the play's questions when they recur transposed, diluted and disguised, in life.[22]

Both the "alienation effect" and the "happening effect" increase distance in Bullough's as well as in Brecht's sense by creating the conditions for a startling new point of view, a larger perspective, though Brook argues that the one attempts to employ reason as the means, the other emotional trauma. This crossing of opposites, by which suddenly heightened closeness shocks the spectator into distance, and suddenly heightened distance is similarly employed to produce personal reflection, is parallel to Wordsworth's and Coleridge's division of all poetry into two parts, one in which Wordsworth makes the familiar strange while in the other Coleridge makes the strange familiar. The departure points are opposed, but it seems that the arrival, epiphany, is the same. Perhaps similarly, drama that *creates* new insights (rather than merely states or explains them) increases distance as a necessary element in that process.

Brook explains that in some happenings, or in theatrical productions that rely on controversial current issues, the response triggered may come too easily and too soon, preventing a more profound experience:

> If the theatre touches a current issue [as in Brook's production of *US* on the Vietnam War] so burning and so uncomfortable as Vietnam it cannot fail to touch off powerful and immediate reactions. This seems a good thing, because we want our theatre to be powerful and immediate. However, when the trigger is so light, when the ejaculation comes so soon, when the first reaction is so strong, it is not possible to go very deep. The shutters fall fast.

With *Oedipus,* a Roman play at a national theatre, all the references are reassuring and so the audience's barriers are down. Hundreds of years of safe and insulated culture make any Oedipus a harmless exercise. So there is no opposition from the audience and it is possible for actors armed with a probing text to go very deeply into the netherlands of human evasion. The audience follows down these dark alleys, calm and confident. Culture is a talisman protecting them from anything that could nastily swing back into their own lives.

The contemporary event touches raw nerves but creates an immediate refusal to listen. The myth and the formally shaped work has power, yet is insulated in exact proportion. So which in fact is more likely to be useful to the spectator? I want to find the answer.[23]

In Brook's view, though dealing with current issues in theatrical productions breaks through initial barriers, reducing the spectator's emotional withdrawal, the response comes too easily, thereby preventing a more sustained emotional response. Presumably, productions using myths and the past provide more distance, meaning more psychological protection because they are more remote from real-world events (political and social) but do have real-world implications (providing insights into human and social behavior). Though Brook finds the immediate effect appealing, he believes that the more remote productions, for example, *Oedipus,* finally create an even deeper experience.

With a parallel example and a similar conclusion, Bullough claims that Greek tragedy is effective today because its "temporal remoteness" reduces practical responses to the work (e.g., to the social and political issues addressed in the play) and therefore provides a protected space in which the spectator's imagination may enter. Because the spectator is less likely to respond practically, that is, in relation to his or her own life, the viewer can have greater appreciation of the "art-character" of the tragedy.

However, Brook, like Sartre, maintains that distance not only permits a greater aesthetic appreciation but allows the spectator to be more intensely involved emotionally.

Happenings, on the other hand, directly "assault" the audience, implicating them immediately in contemporary issues related to the real world. This direct involvement in "reality" in happenings and documentary plays is exactly what Sartre is so concerned about when he describes "the crisis of the imaginary in the theatre." He believes that this constant shifting between the artificial and the real confuses spectators and inhibits their experience of dramatic illusion, presumably by blurring together their awareness of the real and their imaginative involvement in the unreal.

In the later stages of his work, beginning in the 1970s, Grotowski has wanted to move beyond his communication with the audience to something that is even beyond theatre. The "phenomenon called theatre [has become] devoid of meaning" (p. 122) for Grotowski because he is no longer content with the traditional actor-audience division but is attempting to create a new type of communal experience where human beings "meet" together. For Grotowski, even the term "audience" is no longer relevant because he no longer wants distance of any kind, no separation between the performers and the viewers; instead, they are to become "concrete human beings" experiencing a "meeting":

> What part does the audience play? Why worry about what the audience's part ought to be? And what does it really mean "the audience"? We are doing something, and there are others, who want to meet us; some are opening their doors, others come to the meeting, there is something that will happen between us. This is more important than having an idea about the "audience" and its role. (p. 124)

Even the traditional theatre terminology no longer suits Grotowski as he attempts to move beyond the actor-audience division to a "meeting" comparable to religious services. No longer concerned about creating "performances" or events *for* an audience, which would imply a distinction between the roles of performer and perceiver, Grotowski wants everyone assembled to meet on the same plane, thereby making meaningless the distinctions between audience, actors, and performance.

> The words "spectator," "performance," "actor," like the rest of the so-called theatre terminology, I consider anachronistic with regard to what we are looking for.... Years ago we tried to secure a direct participation of spectators. We wanted to have it at any price.... We compelled spectators to "perform" with us.... We reached a point where we rejected these kinds of proceedings, since it was clear that we were exerting pressure, tyranny of sorts. After all, we were putting the people who came to us in a false position, it was disloyal of us: we were prepared for this sort of encounter, while they were not. We were doing it because we wanted to do it; they were doing it because we forced them to do it. And so we told ourselves: no, the spectators should simply be as they are, that is to say, witnesses, witnesses of a human act.... Today I realize that one cannot aim at identifying those who are prepared for the encounter and called actors, with those who are coming for the first time; that no one of those who have come ought to be forced to do anything. But we must be able to prepare the meeting in such a way that a place could be found there for reactions of those who have come, active and passive reactions. (p. 129)

Grotowski has changed his orientation: the lesson he learned was that an audience cannot be forced to participate in a secular rite; so he has abolished the audience, as such. As a consequence he has abolished the theatre, and art, and because a kind of social healing rather than art is his admitted concern, he acknowledges his apostasy.

Now his "meeting" is similar to the theatrical performance of earlier years in an important way: the viewer has the freedom to respond in whatever way he chooses, with "active or passive reactions," but, though he has returned to the voluntary nature of the "audience's" response, he has given up all notion of representation.

> What perspective is opening here? A perspective which transcends acting, with all pretense, with all playing. It is the fullness of man that is thrown onto the scale. A human being in its totality—that is to say what is sensory and at the same time shining through, as it were; soul is

body, body is soul, sex and luminosity. And it would even be difficult to say whether this is physical or psychic, because it is one and the same thing. Acting is simply abandoned. (p. 120)

Attempting to transcend "all pretense," Grotowski is concerned with approaching reality head on—by *presenting* it. No longer creating a fiction to be imaginatively experienced by the viewers, Grotowski has literally decided to establish direct contact with other human beings.

The seed, that act which decides all, that *revealing*, cannot be found through technical perfection, through skill. It is something that is done directly, here and now, or one gives it up. (p. 123)

No longer concerned with theatre, or performance of any kind, Grotowski abandons art as he establishes what seems comparable to group therapy.[24]

We are not concerned any more about something which could be defined as a "work," something stable, fixed, which is suitable for repetition. Everything we are doing now is just a travel outline for a day.... It is only the encounter and its circumstances that are established among ourselves and those who will come to meet us. But the "act" arrived at in the established conditions varies from day to day.... Every day there is a different relation, different communion, different "I see you, I react to you." Different people come to us, and even the participation of those who are close to us is not the same everyday. (p. 132)

His concern is to create opportunities for human beings to reveal themselves to one another. Grotowski's new recognition of the spectator's freedom is in the spirit of democracy, not aesthetics.

Having eliminated the element of unreality in his work, Grotowski has also, of course, done away with aesthetic distance. Grotowski's actors have taken on the role of priests or social psychologists. It is not intended that the spectators view the "encounter" as a created event to be imaginatively experienced, but instead it is to be perceived as a moment in their own lives during which they are trying to discover God or mental health. They are not psychologically protected or emotionally "removed," nor is it desired that they be. Without the element of pretense, of unreality, the "audience" is left with nothing but the real world and each other. Though they are free to respond with "active or passive reactions," they are no longer invited to imagine—to do so would be inappropriate. The result, in Grotowski's own words, "is very serious indeed," and "absolutely without distance."

For Bullough, the ideal degree of distance, which forms the basis of his general aesthetic principle, is the "least amount of distance without its disappearance," and given Sartre's concern with empathic involvement, that would be consistent with Sartre's view. Artaud suggests a radical reduction of distance, but he still wants the spectator to possess the psychological protection implicit in the very situation of knowing that one is in the theatre for the purposes of "serious games." Grotowski, on the other hand, reduces distance to the point of achieving its complete elimination. The removal of the element of unreality leaves the "spectator" unprotected; it is that vulnerability, that willingness to sacrifice privacy, that Grotowski first asked of his actors and has since asked of his participants.

"Reality" functions as a basis for the theories of both Grotowski and Brecht, but they are concerned with vastly different realities and their approaches to that reality are equally different. Brecht is not trying to imitate reality, which consists of abstract social patterns, but tries to maneuver the viewer into insights from which he or she will understand the principles illustrated by his fictions. However untraditional his work may appear, such an orientation permits Brecht to operate within the confines of traditional art.

Grotowski, on the other hand, employs theatre as ritual, and the experience of reality as literal truths; his concern is with an individual, spiritual reality, which, like Brecht's theatre, is a reality that cannot be represented. For Grotowski, theatre is a conversion experience that initiates the spectator into this spiritual reality. But because its first premise is the spectator's trust, vulnerability—in a word, *belief,* as Grotowski gets closer in achieving his objective, he gets further away from theatre and art.

Under normal circumstances, "reality" has no distance, it is perceived and experienced as an existent object. It is only when it is "seen as" something else— to use Wittgenstein's illuminating phrase—that an existent object can at the same moment "be" a nonexistent object. Perhaps the metaphor of distance points to the "space" between the real and the virtual object when something is "seen as." Artaud is too intransigently figurative in his thinking ever to let theatre escape from its double: it is *seen as* ritual, as magic, as surgery, as a plague, etc. He wants to return mankind to its dreams, not to rub its nose in everyday reality. In Grotowski, however, we see that at the point at which distance disappears, so does art: he wants no more pretense. But if the sincerity and truth of art is a product of its "pretense" (our "seeing as"), then the search for sincerity and truth without pretense must take him beyond art.

The "total identification" which sometimes appears as a catchphrase of theorists and theatre artists, if psychologically possible short of insanity, therefore appears to be impossible aesthetically. To literally become one with the object would be to cease to "see as," to cease to sustain distance, to cease to be engaged in an aesthetic experience. Grotowski in his theory and practice seems to illustrate the limits of art and distance.

5

Identification with the Fictional World

The audience's involvement in the imaginary world of fiction is central to many film theorists. The work of Christian Metz and André Bazin is fairly representative of this interest. In addition, their writings reflect a concern with the differences between the theatrical and cinematic experiences. For these film theorists, the relation of the unreal to the real is of prime importance for understanding the qualitative difference in the spectator's experience of theatre and film.

An analysis of the ideas of Metz and Bazin is useful for achieving another angle on the problem: as theorists, their discussions of theatre (as compared with film) come from a different (polemical) point of view. To an important extent, the distinctions they make between theatre and film hinge on notions of distance, making their arguments especially relevant to this study. Therefore, not only do their theories provide insight into the role of distance for the theatre, but by implication they point to the significance of the concept of distance for a more general aesthetic theory.

Describing these spectator experiences in theatre and film, Christian Metz contends that theatre is too "real" in itself to give much impression of reality; therefore the viewer can more fully engage in a fictional world in the film than in the theatre:

> The actor's bodily presence contradicts the temptation one always experiences during the show to perceive him as a protagonist in a fictional universe, and the theatre can only be a freely accepted game played among accomplices. Because the theatre is too real, theatrical fictions yield only a weak impression of reality.... The impression of reality we get from a film does not depend at all on the strong presence of an actor but rather on the low degree of existence possessed by those ghostly creatures moving on the screen, and they are, therefore, unable to resist our constant impulse to invest them with the "reality" of fiction..., a reality that comes only from within us, from the projections and identifications that are mixed in our perception of film. The film spectacle produces a strong impression of reality because it corresponds to a "vacuum, which dreams readily fill."[1]

Metz is here contending that because the theatre spectator perceives a real actor, and is quite aware of the individual *as* actor, the viewer must consciously accept the event before him or her as merely a "game played among accomplices." Implied in that view is the notion that film is *more* than a "game," that on some fundamental level it does not require as much conscious complicity between film and spectator. In addition, Metz contends that in theatre the spectator is more aware of the actual reality of the theatre (scenery, props, actual space), making it much more difficult for the "reality" of the fiction to take form. In theatre, the spectator is much more aware of the theatrical representation itself, causing the object of the representation, that is, the fictional universe, to recede, primarily leaving the perception of the real rather than the illusion of the unreal. In film, however, Metz believes that because the spectator is not so consciously aware of the real bodily presence of the actors (due to their "low degree of existence"), he or she can experience the fictional world in its own right, as its own "reality." Because film is like a "vacuum," providing few obstacles to the imaginative engagement of the spectator, it makes it easier for the viewer to "project" into, and identify with, the fictional universe.

Because of their different media of presentation, film and theatre, in Metz's view, significantly differ in their ability to create a fictional world for the spectator. The "real" in theatre disrupts the fictional universe: "It is quite obvious that when a stage actor sneezes or hesitates in his delivery the brutal interruption by 'real' reality disrupts the reality of the fiction." Film, on the other hand, "dismisses this set of resistances and levels all obstacles to spectator participation" because the real world "does not intrude upon the fiction and constantly deny its claim to reality."[2] In the theatre, though, the spectator is not able to experience the "illusion" because "the element that is more powerful in the theatre is not the 'illusion' of reality but *reality itself.* . . . The spectator no longer has the illusion of reality; he has the perception of reality—he is a witness to real events."[3]

Like Bullough and Sartre, Metz believes that the spectator projects onto the fictional object, but Metz thinks the viewer is more capable of doing this in film where the medium reduces the interference with such imaginative engagements. When he likens film to a "vacuum, which dreams readily fill," Metz contends that film creates the condition (he even suggests a compulsion) for the spectator to imaginatively engage in the unreal aesthetic object. Film as a medium is characterized by Metz as creating the least possible distance because the unreality of the film images does not intrude upon the fictional world, thereby compelling the viewer into engagement. Theatre, on the other hand, presumably creates too much distance, making it difficult for the viewer to imagine the nonexistent fictional object. The means of the representation— real actors, props, scenery, and actual space—and therefore the perception of the real, often overpowers the imagination.

Metz attempts to more specifically deal with film's impression of reality and the spectator's "projection" into the "vacuum" by rigorously analyzing the ontological status of the film image as signifier.[4] Metz maintains that even though fictional theatre and fictional film involve an imaginary world, the fictional film is even more fictional because the "unfolding" itself is fictive, whereas the theatre involves real time, space, and people.

> The perceptions that theatre and other spectacles offer to the eye and the ear are inscribed in a true space (not a photographed one), the same one as that occupied by the public during the performance; everything the audience hear and see is actively produced in their presence, by human beings or props which are themselves present. This is not the problem of fiction but that of the definitional characteristics of the signifier: whether or not the theatrical play mimes a fable, its *action*, if need be mimetic, is still managed by real persons evolving in real time and space, *on the same stage or "scene" as the public.* The "other scene," which is precisely not so called, is the cinematic screen (closer to fantasy from the outset): what unfolds there may, as before, be more or less fiction, but the unfolding itself is fictive: the actor, the "decor," the words one hears are all absent, everything is *recorded* (as a memory trace which is immediately so, without having been something else before), and this is still true if what is recorded is not a "story" and does not aim for the fictional illusion proper. For it is the signifier itself, and as a whole, that is recorded, that is absence.[5]

Here Metz is taking his comparison of the *means* of representation in theatre and film a step further. Because the representation on the cinematic screen consists of a mere "recording" of events which have taken place elsewhere, the images themselves, as signifiers of a fictional world, manifest "absence." "The unfolding itself is fictive" in that actual space, real actors, and the "decor" have all been removed from the filmic spectacle, leaving the spectator with only a "trace" of the real. Theatre's means of representation, however, are, in Metz's explanation, fundamentally different: real actors, props, and actual space are continually present in the spectator's perception of the theatrical spectacle.

In Metz's theory, theatre and film significantly differ because in theatre the spectator actually sees a chair, whereas in film only the *reflection* of a chair. In theatre, the audience perceives a real actor, whereas in film sees only a "shadow" of an actor.

> At the theatre, Sarah Bernhardt may tell me she is Phèdre or, if the play were from another period and rejected the figurative regime, she might say, as in a type of modern theatre, that she is Sarah Bernhardt. But at any rate, I should see Sarah Bernhardt. At the cinema, she could make the same two kinds of speeches too, but it would be her shadow that would be offering them to me (or she would be offering them in her own absence). Every film is a fiction film. (p. 47)

In the fiction film the signifier is more or less transparent as it "removes the traces of its own steps." Although Metz seems to fully accept a distance concept and the notion of art as a known fiction, he implies that minimal distance is primarily inherent to the film medium, and that film's superiority is based on that reduced distance which allows intense engagement with an unreal fictional object. For Metz, the sense of absence fully characterizes our spectator involvement with the film event: we receive a greater impression of reality, and are better able to identify (than we can in theatre) because we perceive the photographed object as absent, the photograph as present, and "the presence of this absence as signifying" (p. 58). The greater reality in the presence of this absence is exactly comparable to Sartre's view (as exemplified in the Genet anecdote, for instance) that filling that vacuum with one's own imagination makes that imagined reality one's own, and therefore more real to one (the only reality being the one that each of us owns).

Metz believes that cinema is better able to create identification because the dual character of film's signifying process involves us more in the imaginary.

> The unique position of cinema lies in this dual character of its signifier: unaccustomed perceptual wealth, but unusually profoundly stamped with unreality, from its very beginning. More than the other arts, or in a more unique way, the cinema involves us in the imaginary: it drums up all perception, but to switch it immediately over into its absence, which is nonetheless the only signifier present. (p. 48)

In Metz's view, because the film has access to the world—all of nature can be photographed—it is characterized as possessing "unaccustomed perceptual wealth." But because the film images are only "recordings" of these perceptions, they are characterized by "absence": "perceptual wealth" is switched over to the unreality of the film images' "absence."

Metz's description of the perceptual experience of film is comparable to Bullough's notion of "switching on a current"—a perceptual transformation of the object. In a similar way, Sartre maintains that we perceive the real but then consciousness undergoes a "radical change in which the world is negated": perceiving is switched to an imaginative consciousness (imaging). But Metz seems to specifically reject an either/or exclusivity of perceiving and imaging. In saying that the medium itself is fictive, even if the subject matter is real and there is no aim for "fictional illusion," as in the documentary film, Metz is contending that film creates a simultaneity of the real and the fictional, that is, perceiving and imaging fuse in the spectator's experience of the film.

Whereas Metz locates the "absence" in the actual film image—it is only a "recording"—Sartre places the unreality in the mind of the perceiver. For Sartre, the spectator perceives real objects (even real actors in the theatre), but then the viewer's consciousness (not the representation or the "signifier") switches over to an imaginative attitude: imaging an unreal aesthetic object.

André Bazin expresses a similar point of view to that of Metz's when he explains in "Theatre and Cinema" that in the theatre we are too aware of the actor to be able to identify with the fictional character. Bazin quotes Rosenkrantz, who wrote in 1937 in *Esprit:*

> The characters on the screen are quite naturally objects of identification, while those on the stage are, rather, objects of mental opposition because their real presence gives them an objective reality and to transpose them into beings in an imaginary world the will of the

spectator has to intervene actively, that is to say, to will to transform their physical reality into an abstraction. This abstraction being the result of a process of the intelligence that we can only ask of a person who is fully conscious.[6]

Like Metz, Bazin also states that theatre requires a conscious recognition of real actors and actual space, which prevents (or significantly limits) an imaginative involvement with the unreal fictional world. The spectator is presumably so aware of the real actor as performer that he or she must "intervene actively" with a conscious will to simultaneously imagine that person as a nonexistent character. Bazin implies that film, on the other hand, does not require the conscious "will of the spectator" to transform the images on the screen into characters with whom to identify. In fact, Bazin goes on to explicitly state that the spectator's experiences of theatre and film significantly differ due to theatre's reliance on convention.

> Illusion in the cinema is not based as it is in the theatre on convention tacitly accepted by the general public; rather, contrariwise, it is based on the inalienable realism of that which is shown. All trick work must be perfect in all material respects on the screen. (p. 108)

For Bazin, the power of film is not that it is based on conventions accepted by the viewers, but that its "realism," which "follows directly from its photographic nature," allows the spectator to directly experience that which takes place on the screen, almost as if the spectator were perceiving the real world. Here Bazin is explicitly stating that film does not require the acceptance of convention because it is based on "inalienable realism": similar to the world, film is presumably perceived in the same way as the real world.[7]

Bazin further distinguishes between theatre and film by comparing their differing uses of space.[8] According to Bazin, theatre is in direct contrast with the rest of the world: "play and reality are opposed."

> Theatre of its very essence must not be confused with nature under penalty of being absorbed by her and ceasing to be. Founded on the reciprocal awareness of those taking part and present to one another, it must be in contrast to the rest of the world in the same way the play and reality are opposed.... Costume, mask, or make-up, the style of the language, the footlights, all contribute to the stage, the architecture of which has varied from time to time without ever ceasing to mark out a privileged spot actually or virtually distinct from nature. It is precisely in virtue of this *locus dramaticus* that decor exists. It serves in greater or less degree to set the place apart, to specify. (p. 104)

Theatre, because it employs real people and real objects set within actual space, must create a direct opposition to the real world and Bazin suggests that the spectator is always aware of this opposition. Bazin is actually describing the conditions for distance in the theatre: the theatrical event is not confused with nature; actors and audience share a "reciprocal awareness"; and theatre is characterized by its artificial devices (costumes, make-up, lighting, etc.).

Film, on the other hand, is apparently not opposed to real life because its basic principle is "a denial of any frontiers to action." The film exists on a continuum with the space of the rest of the world:[9]

> The idea of *locus dramaticus* is not only alien to, it is essentially a contradiction of the concept of the screen. The screen is not a frame like that of a picture but a mask which allows only part of the action to be seen. When a character moves off screen, we accept the fact that he is out of sight, but he continues to exist in his own capacity at some other place in the decor which is hidden from us. There are no wings to the screen. There could not be without destroying its specific illusion. (p. 105)

Rejecting the analogy that film is like a frame, Bazin is actually contending that film is a window on reality. Therefore, when a character moves off screen, "we accept the fact" that he continues to exist, though out of our sight, in the "other" space of the world, the space "which is hidden from us." When Bazin contends that "there are no wings to the screen" and "could not be without destroying its specific illusion," he seems to imply that the cinematic illusion is actually the reality of the world, or, more specifically, "only part of the action" in the real world.

Presumably, because of film's more intimate relation to the real world, it is, in Bazin's view, able to substitute for the space of the real world.

> The world of the screen and our world cannot be juxtaposed. The screen of necessity substitutes for it since the very concept of universe is spatially exclusive. For a time, a film is the Universe, the world, of if you like, Nature. (pp. 108-9)

Rather than the spectator creating an alternate universe from the film's fiction, or accepting the fictional world as a metaphor for the real world, the viewer presumably allows the film to "substitute" for the world. Instead of experiencing the imaginative tension between the fictional world and the real world, the spectator, in Bazin's theory, experiences "the world of the screen" as a replacement for reality.

In a later essay, "An Aesthetic of Reality: Neorealism," Bazin presents a more sophisticated view of the nature of convention in the film, allowing that "realism in art can only be achieved in one way—through artifice." He says that cinema lives off the contradiction between its attempt to create an "illusion of reality" and its current inability to present reality (which would not be art in any case). But though Bazin here admits the existence, even the necessity for conventions and abstraction in film, he sees them as corrosives which threaten to dissolve "authentic reality." (In Bazin's thinking there can be "inauthentic realities"—illusions, self-consistent systems, abstractions, or whatever else may achieve levels of credibility but do not return the spectator to "reality" as Bazin conceives it.) Reality, which Bazin never clearly defines, remains his touchstone: "One might group, if not classify in order of importance, the various styles of cinematography in terms of the added measure of reality."[10] Thus the artifice which he admits to, the presence of what he calls abstraction and convention in cinematic art that he accepts as necessities, are not, for Bazin, positive values nor even neutral qualities of the medium: they are necessary evils, perhaps only temporary functions of an evolving technology. The value of film continues to inhere in its "reality," and his admissions of unreal elements in film serve only to warn film-makers against becoming "dupes" of their *art* (presumably no warning is needed against becoming a dupe of authentic reality).

Bazin's ideas about film's physical similarity to the real world, and the spatial exclusivity of film and the real world, allow him to describe film as if it is merely a segment of the actual world: it is "but a mask which allows only part of the action to be seen." Therefore, if a character moves off the screen, he or she continues to exist (even though not seen) in the world of the film, which is compatible with the space of the world. The character of the film apparently does not step off into a "wing," but, in Bazin's view, the character simply steps into a continuation of the film.

Yet it is not quite clear, from Bazin's statements, how this "existence" of the fictional character differs for theatre and film. In theatre, the actor continues to live, and is understood to do so, when he or she steps into the wing. More important, the fictional character in theatre continues to exist for the audience even when not seen. Only the actors in theatre step into the wings; characters move into other fictional places. "We accept the fact," he says, that "when a character moves off screen . . . he is out of sight, but . . . continues to exist." Of course that *fact* is merely an illusion; a character has no existence outside the art object except in our imagination. Like a character in a novel, only when the vehicle for that character exists does the character exist. In other words, it is not because the character has some kind of reality that is independent of the film and part of a larger reality that "we accept the fact" of a continuous off-screen existence but because "we accept the fact" of narrative convention and, within that, of screen convention. We equally accept the fact that Bugs Bunny will return to befuddle Elmer Fudd as we do that Cary Grant will return to the screen to embrace Grace Kelly. It is not the reality of the actor nor of the decor that creates this illusion but that willingness to suspend *dis*belief according to the rules, which is part of every theatrical convention.

According to Bazin, cinema's unique use of space creates an intense psychological engagement that involves a sense of presence just as much as the theatre creates a sense of presence with its use of real space.[11] Bazin suggests that because there are no wings to the screen, we actually have access, as film spectators, to the entire space of the world: a partial recording, film accounts for part of the world but always indicates the space beyond.

Although Bazin recognizes that a film is an artificially constructed object produced by a film-maker (that it "opens upon an artificial world"), he emphasizes that it is the film's connection to the real world that creates the spectator's intense psychological identification in film. Bazin contends that because of the "objective nature" of the photographic image, it possesses "a quality of credibility absent from all other picture-making." As perceiver, "we are forced to accept as real the existence of the object reproduced, actually *re-presented*.... Photography enjoys a certain advantage in virtue of this transference of reality from the thing to its reproduction."[12] Because so little comes between actual reality and the perception of reality in "its reproduction," the spectator supposedly experiences an intense engagement with the film images. Because the viewer is presumably not conscious of the "reality" of the actor as actor, nor of the film as film, he or she can perceive the film with very little distance, with minimal awareness of fiction or artificiality. In Bazin's view, the spectator experiences the film *as* reality, and therefore invests in the fictional characters.[13] In theatre, however, the real space of the theatre building is vividly set apart from the space of the real world; the separation of space causes us to relate more to the actors than to identify with the characters.

Metz also thinks that the spectator more easily identifies in film, but for Metz, due to the imaginary nature of film's signifier, its inherently minimal degree of distance, the film spectator identifies with the entire filmic event. For Metz, film-viewing is a "semi-oneiric instance" and the spectator-screen relationship like a mirror identification,[14] though the film is different from the mirror in "one essential point": the spectator's own body is never reflected on the screen. Asking himself the question, "*With what,* then, does the spectator identify during the projection of the film?" (p. 49), Metz arrives at a solution: the spectator identifies him or herself as "all-perceiving subject" (knowing that he or she has made the images coherent, that he or she has, in a sense, "made" the film). This supposed identification with self (as the infant identifies with his own image in the mirror) means that "the spectator can do no other than identify with the camera" (p. 52), because otherwise we could not explain certain facts—like why the spectator is not amazed when the image rotates. In other words, the minimal degree of distance inherent to the perception of film presumably prevents a noticeable awareness of film techniques, thereby allowing for a continual imaginative involvement with the film images— identification with the entire film event.

Here again Metz's ideas are quite similar to those of Sartre, as well as those of Bullough. Both Sartre and Bullough maintain that distance allows a projection of our emotions onto the object outside ourselves, and for Sartre, this projection creates a semblance of belief in the object. Metz, on the other hand, maintains that the minimal distance allows the film spectator to project onto the screen in a manner analogous to the young infant's projection during the Lacanian "mirror-phase": just as the infant perceives a coherent image in the mirror,[15] the spectator makes the film images coherent through his own type of "mirror identification." Not unlike Bullough and Sartre (though his psychoanalytic vocabulary differs radically), Metz contends that the spectator actually completes the fiction within his or her own mind.

Both Metz and Bazin argue that the very presence of real actors who are *aware* of the spectator's presence prevents identification in the theatre. In theatre, the audience and actor share a reciprocal awareness of one another, yet, as Bazin points out, in cinema, just the opposite occurs:

> Hidden in a dark room, we watch through half-open blinds a spectacle that is unaware of our existence.... There is nothing to prevent us from identifying ourselves in imagination with the moving world before us, which becomes *the* world. (p. 102)

Because the film is unaware of our existence, we are presumably more protected from the event, more sheltered in the "dark room," and this protected vulnerability allows the viewer to identify with the characters in the film's fictional world. Here both Metz and Bazin are claiming that the distance inherent to the film experience itself—the unreality of the film images and the film's lack of awareness of its audience—creates a psychological protection that allows for an intense imaginative involvement with the unreal fictional universe "which becomes *the* world."

Although both Metz and Bazin agree that such intense imaginative engagement primarily occurs in film and not in theatre, their reasons for holding such a view are radically different. Bazin is concerned with *actual* reality:[16] the film spectator perceptually and imaginatively responds due to film's special connection to the real world and its "objective" nature.[17] Metz, on the other hand, thinks that intense imaginative involvement occurs during the entire filmic event because film creates an "*impression* of reality" due to the fictive nature (the unreal quality) of the film images. In Metz's "The Impression of Reality," he compares the impression of reality in photography, film, and theatre:

> The truth is that there seems to be an optimal point, film, on either side of which the impression of reality produced by the fiction tends to decrease. On the one side, there is the theatre, whose too real vehicle puts fiction to flight; on the other, photography and representational painting, whose means are too poor in their degree of reality to constitute and sustain a diegetic universe. If it is true that one does not believe in the reality of a dramatic intrigue because the theatre is too real, it is also true that one does not believe in the reality of the photographed object—because the rectangle of paper (grayish, scant, and motionless) is *not real enough*. A representation bearing too few allusions to reality does not have sufficient *indicative* force to give body to its fictions; a representation constituting total reality, as in the case of the theatre, thrusts itself on perception as something real trying to imitate something unreal, and not as a realization of the unreal. Between these two shoals, film sails a narrow course: It carries enough elements of reality—the literal translation of graphic contours and, mainly, the real presence of motion—to furnish us with rich and varied information.... The total reality of the spectacle is greater in the theatre than in motion pictures, but the portion of reality available to the fiction is greater in the cinema than in the theatre.[18]

Here Metz directly reveals his reliance on an implied concept of distance as he examines the relationship of the unreal to the real, maintaining that one can only experience "the impression of reality," and the fictional world, if the object represents reality to the "optimal" degree. For Metz, theatre is too real for imaginative involvement; the perception of reality intrudes upon the dramatic illusion. The theatrical experience involves too much distance because the spectator so consciously perceives—and is imaginatively limited by—the real world of the theatre. In addition, the perception of photography, even more so than theatre, involves too much distance because it "is not real enough," "bearing too few allusions to reality" such as movement and size to provide the image enough guidance or "*indicative* force." Unable to provide a sufficient resemblance to reality, the photography cannot create "the impression of reality" and the reduced distance in the viewer that allow for intense imaginative engagement. Film, however, with its access to the real world and the unreality ("absence") of its signifier, can presumably create an intense impression of reality, and thereby a consistently minimal degree of distance, that allow for a continual and sustained imaginative involvement with the fiction.

In one sense Metz seems to imply that distance involves an awareness of conventions which create the artificiality of the event. For this reason Metz sees theatre as being much more convention-bound than film. Due to the physical presence of the actors on the stage, the spectator may easily become conscious of the real actors and objects *as* real persons and objects. The spectator must enter into a conspiracy (a convention) that permits real persons and things to be seen fictively; but the reality of the actor drags the imagination down, constantly threatening to eliminate distance as the spectator sees the actor as real human being. Film, in Metz's view, has an unalterable minimum degree of distance—distance can never be totally nullified. The unreality of the film images does not intrude upon the illusion; therefore the spectator can more easily imaginatively engage with the fictional world. In this sense Metz conceives of this minimum degree of distance inherent in the perception of film as allowing for the imaginative involvement in the unreal aesthetic object. Whereas Sartre locates the unreality in the consciousness of the spectator (who "images" the unreal aesthetic object), Metz moves in another direction when he locates that unreality in the film image itself, which, as "signifier," manifests "absence." In this way, Metz sees the film experience as manifesting, as Bullough phrases it, "the least amount of distance without its disappearance," resulting in the spectator's "identification" with the entire filmic event.

Bazin also suggests that the film more easily engages the spectator because of film's minimum degree of distance but goes even further than Metz by advocating those films "closest" to reality. With films using "invisible montage" and "depth of focus," the spectator supposedly relates to the space of the film in the same way that he or she relates to the space of the world, with no noticeable "translation" from one experience to the other, and with very little awareness of the real world: the viewer perceives the images *as* reality. Bazin's preference for neorealistic films reflects his interest in the perception of the "fullness of the universe." Without quite reaching the extreme of implying that the perception of film involves no distance, no awareness of the distinction between reality and film, Bazin does contend that the ideal films, most especially the neorealistic films, achieve such limited and subtle uses of devices that the films are perceived *as* reality.

When Bazin maintains that the characters on the stage are "objects of mental opposition" because "to transpose them into beings in an imaginary world the will of the spectator has to intervene actively," he implies in his comparison that there is little in the film or the surrounding movie theatre to make the viewer conscious that he or she is watching a film. And when Bazin states that theatre relies on convention while film relies on illusion, he is implying that as spectator, the viewer is aware of the artificiality of the event in the theatre, its use of conventions, whereas in film the spectator primarily perceives the images as if they are just a continuation of the real space of the world. Though conventions are used, they create an "illusion of reality." In other words, Metz is insisting that the film spectator's minimal distance results from the unreality of the film images; Bazin claims that the film spectator's radically reduced distance occurs while perceiving films which are most like the real world (without noticeable film techniques to "manipulate" the film viewer).

The difficulty with Bazin's point of view is that it greatly limits the value of films which exploit the complicity between the object and the viewer. Film, too, is but a game, even though the conditions of the game-playing may be more deceptive than those in the theatre. Yet film also relies on the acceptance of certain rules or "conventions," as Metz points out in his "The Fiction Film and Its Spectator." Metz explains that the film spectator agrees to play the game of film-viewing and accepts in advance to conduct himself as spectator.[19] To experience the "fiction-effect," the spectator must adopt a particular *visée de conscience.*[20]

Though film is obviously physically different from theatre (the movie theatre is usually darker; there is less applause; the actors are not present in the same space as the audience; etc.), the difference in the spectator's awareness of the work as "artificial," his distance from the work, is really one of differing degress, not of opposition. During both, the sane spectator has to be aware that he or she is perceiving a film or theatrical production, and not genuine "reality." In both instances, the spectator agrees to accept a representation as a vehicle to experience a nonexistent fictional world. In other words, some degree of distance is intrinsic to the perception of both film and theatre, though film may indeed, as Metz maintains, more easily achieve reduced distance: its "impression of reality" may easily create imaginative involvement.

Although Metz's argument deals with the ontological nature of film itself, the medium's relation to reality, his analysis in "Imaginary Signifier" is limited to the extent that he only discusses the classical Hollywood film (which presumably removes "the traces of its own steps"). Though wanting to describe the "essence" of cinema (its inherently minimum degree of distance), he limits the discussion to one particular kind of film.[21]

As Mary Anne Doane points out, even these classical Hollywood films do not hide the work of their production,[22] but rather a significant number of films are "dialogical."[23] Even the classical Hollywood film that Metz cites as being the ultimate of the fictional film in removing "the traces of its own steps," thereby creating minimal distance, involves a complicity between the viewer and the film. As Stephen Heath in "Narrative Space" emphasizes, classical cinema does not make the signs of production "invisible," for the film is a series of relations with the spectator that it imagines; the experience of the actual process of production, that is, conventions and devices, is very important to the filmic event.[24] And as Mitry maintains, the real itself has no double and can therefore never be art; filmic conventions distance as film splits itself off from the real world and becomes a discourse on the world.[25]

Both Metz and Bazin imply that the film experience has an inherent minimal distance when they maintain that the film-viewing experience is voyeuristic, as evident in Bazin's insistence that theatre involves the bodily presence of actors who are aware of the audience's existence, whereas film does not:

> Hidden in a dark room we watch through half-open blinds a spectacle that is unaware of our existence.... There is nothing to prevent us from identifying ourselves in imagination with the moving world before us, which becomes *the* world. (p. 102)

This lack of awareness of another's presence is often treated in contemporary film theory in terms of voyeurism: with the film actor unaware of our presence, we voyeuristically perceive the events on the screen, feeling protected by the distance between ourselves and the fictional world. Supposedly isolated in the dark movie theatre, we can view the imaginary "world" projected on the screen without it being aware of our desire to view, or of our act of perception.

Yet, as Doane points out, the difficulty with relying on this psychoanalytical vocabulary is that it takes only part of the package: Freud always discussed voyeurism in light of the opposite tendency, exhibitionism. Both Bazin and Metz deny the exhibitionism of the film when they claim that the actor is unaware of the spectator's presence. Yet, the important matter is not the viewer's relation to the actor but his or her relation to the film, and the film *is* essentially aware of the spectator's presence. A "contract" is made between film and spectator before the film begins, involving a complicity between the film itself and the viewer.[26]

Metz and Bazin's concern that the actors in film not be aware of the presence of the audience is somewhat similar to Sartre's comments on the direct address device in the theatre. For Sartre, the actor directly addressing the audience causes the imaginary character to disappear, destroying the spectator's distanced involvement:

> In the theatre the "someone else" never looks at me; or should he happen to look at me, then the actor, the imaginary character, vanishes. Hamlet or Volpone vanishes and it is Barrault or Dullin looking at me. What is wrong with addressing an audience is that it causes the imaginary character to vanish and to be replaced by the presence of the real person.[27]

Sartre is concerned that the spectator's aesthetic distance not be destroyed as it would if he or she became aware of the real as only real, the actor as person and not as the nonexistent being in the spectator's imagination.

The important point in this comparison with Sartre's ideas is not that the film actor or the theatre actor is unaware of the audience, but that either or both can "avert their eyes" and "pretend" to be only the character who is unaware of the devices of either theatre or film. Of course, both the film actor and the theatre actor can also demonstrate their awareness of the audience and the constraints of the medium within which they are working by drawing attention to the filmic conventions, or to the theatrical devices. The difference, then, between the film actor's and the theatre actor's awareness of the audience is that the film actor can only relate to a generalized audience, whereas the theatre performer responds to a specific, live audience.

Bazin contends that in the theatre one cannot imaginatively engage with the characters because the bodily presence of the actors requires the conscious "will of the spectator" to overcome their physicality. Sartre, on the other hand, maintains that all imagining, no matter what the medium or the type of object or event which stimulates it, is voluntary and requires "a fully spontaneous consciousness" that is "fully free." Unlike Bazin and Metz's contention that the theatre spectator has difficulty overcoming the bodily presence of the theatre actors, Sartre's theory of the imagination does not limit the imagination's capacity to "overcome" physical aspects of objects (such as real actors in the theatre) but insists that the mind is free to image a nonexistent aesthetic object when stimulated by an actual object.

In a similar way to Sartre's theory that the aesthetic experience occurs when perception ceases, when the real is negated, for Metz (and for Bullough) perception shifts from a reality (or pragmatic) to an aesthetic (or image-making) mode of thinking. Here Metz and Sartre use remarkably similar vocabularies in their emphasis on the unreality element. Sartre states that "the real serves to create unreality" and that the event "reveals its *absence*" whereas Metz emphasizes that the film image itself manifests absence, for it, too, is fictive. And for Sartre, the ideal level of distance involves the least possible impediment to the imagination after it is stimulated, which is also similar to Metz, for whom "reality" does not intrude upon the perception of the film to impede the imagination.

When describing the happening and the documentary plays, Sartre maintains that real confrontations create a need for a protective distance, and the direct assault on the audience in these contemporary forms of theatre creates a "crisis of the imaginary," as one's selfhood is threatened in direct contact with another human being. Metz takes this a step further: for him, any bodily presence of actors in a theatre automatically impedes imaginative involvement. For Sartre, the averted eyes of the fictional character permits the spectator to be an observer and therefore to merge imaginatively. But for Metz those averted eyes can only be experienced through the "ghostly creatures" on the screen, who can truly look at the spectator.

For Sartre, the spectator is drawn to share the character's feelings because those feelings are "owned" by the spectator. In a similar way, Metz believes we identify with the events on the screen as a type of "mirror identification": the spectator lends coherence to the film images, and hence identifies with the objects there, because the viewer, in a sense, "owns" them—that is, creates them.

For Metz, intense imaginative involvement and a minimum awareness of the fictionality of the event are characteristic of the "essence" of film, whereas for Sartre, these are the functions of all arts in achieving the highest aesthetic principles.

Perhaps Metz's greatest contribution to our understanding of the concept of distance is that involvement with the art object is made easier when "fictionality" (nonreality) is inherent in the medium itself: Bullough's Paradox is as fundamental to film as it is to theatre (or to other art forms). Both the novel and the film have a built-in fictionality (neither use realities to represent nonrealities). But this comparison also suggests the limited usefulness of Metz's observation: "decoding" the film to experience its fictional world need not stimulate the imagination to any noticeable degree (though, of course, films can be created to stimulate the imagination by inducing high-level interpretations). Perhaps the apparent easiness, the greater accessibility of film, lies not in the nonreality of its ghostly shadows but in their verisimilitude, as Bazin argues: we can relax in front of a moving window that opens on reality. But it is not reality itself that we are seeing, as Metz argues and we know, nor is there an absence of convention in the act of witnessing films. Perhaps, then, the apparent ease with which film is entered is not so much that it is inherently fictive (both theatre-going and film-going involve conventions) but the degree of *passivity* of the spectator. In both novel-reading and theatre-going, high-level translations of what is before the perceiver's eyes are fundamental and necessary to make any sense of what is going on. Only low-level mental activity seems *necessary* to the film experience (though obviously some specific films greatly challenge mental activity).

The novel and film, however, share a different attribute: they make the creation of point of view easy (in both, eliminating point of view is difficult).[28] In theatre, however, the creation of point of view is difficult; theatre has been classically known as the objective art form. Whereas in the novel, someone tells the story (whether in first or third person); in the film, the camera points the viewer where to look, thereby directing perception and enforcing a point of view;[29] in theatre, however, though the director can draw attention to specific aspects of the production, it is more difficult to control the perceptual activity of the spectator for the purpose of creating point of view. When the actor steps upstage center, the audience tends to notice him, but the movement does not necessarily express a particular orientation to the fictional character or to the play as a whole. Although various directorial decisions can force (or encourage) the viewer to focus on particular characters or activities onstage, it is difficult to control the various physical elements in the theatre to enforce a point of view toward the work, though all good directors aspire to create that forceful "voice," a particular "vision" of the play.

But it could be argued that this "identification" with the point of view of the storyteller and the camera creates a "friction" that the imagination must overcome in order for identification to take place with the characters *in* the story or film. In other words, some independence from this point of view may, at times, be necessary to fully "identify" with the characters from their "internal" perspectives.[30] This friction between "identification" with the author or camera's point of view and identification with the characters in the film or the novel, is perhaps the counterpart of the friction created by theatre's heightened awareness of the bodily presence of actors. Indeed, it could be argued that it is precisely that friction in all forms of art and the mental effort required to overcome it, that constitutes an aspect of distance. The theatre spectator imaginatively overcomes, at times, the physical presence of the actors to "see" them as characters (unreality is created from reality); the film-goer and the reader of the novel imaginatively overcome point of view to "see" the character "internally," that is, as he or she exists in the fictional world (separate from the judgments of that character as expressed in the point of view).

It may be argued, then, that film has an advantage over theatre initially in creating a minimum degree of distance because it is more fictive as a medium— at least more obviously—than theatre. Real human beings are not necessarily fictive or, indeed, usually fictive; in the theatre the real must be "seen as" the unreal by the spectator. But the initial advantage of film may in no way compensate for the imaginative loss sustained: if—as Bullough and Sartre suggest—the perceivers in theatre must employ greater will to overcome the literalness of the actor, it may be that their imaginative involvement will be all the more intense and with greater imaginative range as a result of the struggle for perception. The range of images that can be placed before the theatre spectator is not greater; film can present images to an extent that theatre cannot match. Even Metz's argument suggests that film images *precipitate* the imagination: a kind of condensation of imagination fills in the absence created by the film image with the substantiality it lacks. Sartre, however, argues that the very substantiality of the theatre image forces the imagination to fill its absence with insubstantial acts of consciousness that may have no real counterparts, that cannot be depicted or expressed or evoked in any other way. Metz's concept of "absence" is much less evocative than Sartre's. For Sartre the recognition of an absence in an object frees the imagination, permitting it to conceive of images not literally related to the object. Compared with Sartre's theory of negation, Metz's notion is impoverished, almost a modern theory of imitation: the intangibility of the projected shadows provokes the spectator to make the film images concrete in his imagination. Moreover, Metz's "absence," unlike Sartre's, does not emphasize the spectator's awareness or volition; the spectator is relatively passive.

If Metz's polemical purpose to urge the superiority of film over other art forms is distinguished from his fundamental premises, he can be seen to reinforce the views of Bullough and Sartre. While his particular application of those principles to the distinction between film and theatre are arguable, their similarity to those of Bullough and Sartre is clear. Metz is especially useful in extrapolating the notion of aesthetic "projection," which appears in both Bullough's and Sartre's theories: it is "the low degree of existence" of the characters (e.g., our awareness that Hamlet exists as a fictional character) that makes our concept of those characters unable to resist "our constant impulse to invest them with the 'reality' of fiction. . . , a reality that comes from within us." In other words, as Sartre points out, it is some part of ourselves that is invested in a particular fictional character, and Metz makes clear, what is perhaps implicit in Sartre's view, that the character has no defenses against our invasion.

However, the greater refinement of Metz's theory permits us, as usual, to see the weaknesses implicit in it. In traditional theatre the Punch and Judy Show and in film the animated dots illustrate rather extreme cases of "characters" with quite low levels of existence and therefore little resistance to our investment of a fictional reality in them. And, indeed, they do illustrate Metz's point; but what is surprising, given Metz's theory, is that we invest so little reality in them. If low existence were the key to identification, the moving dots on the screen would have the capacity to become "Super-Hamlets"—but that seems quite unlikely. The "low level of existence" in these cases translates into a high level of distance. When seen in those terms it becomes apparent that Metz is thinking comparatively, not absolutely. It is only in comparison with the presence of living actors that the "ghostly creatures moving on the screen" have a low level of existence, but once it is granted that they are only two-dimensional images, in all other ways, the characters may have every attribute of living human beings.

The combination, then, of unreality with recognizable human characteristics seems to be the minimum requirement for identification, and both of these conditions are variable and provide the borders within which distance operates. Those qualities that make the object seem like ourselves (humanization) pull the object toward us; those aspects which distinguish the object from ourselves and our real world (an awareness of fictionality) push the object away from us. The aesthetic tension between these two opposing tendencies constitutes distance and provides the conditions for the variability of distance: as Bullough explains, distance involves a personal relationship with the object, on the one hand, and the object's dissociation from the practical world of reality, on the other. Bullough's ideal, then, "the least amount of distance without its disappearance," is the most intense personal relationship with the art object with a sufficient awareness of its fictionality to prevent practical responses.

The most intense personal relationship with a minimum awareness of fictionality is "low" distance and the combination that the realistic film and realistic play aspire to. An increased awareness of fiction combined with the lowest humanization is largely the province of farce in the theatre, of Punch and Judy, and stylized theatre of extreme abstraction. The combination of a high (but varying) perception of unreality and a high (but varying) humanization is the corner occupied by Brecht in such plays as *Mother Courage*. And probably no "dramatic" medium better combines high awareness of fictionality and low humanization so well as the films that experiment with moving dots.

Though our perception of unreality and humanization vary in different *types* of plays, the conditions of distance are also variable within any given play. For instance, Chekhov's *The Cherry Orchard* generally employs conditions for low awareness of unreality and high humanization, but at various moments in the play the conditions shift for dramatic effect. In the final scene of the play, Gaev and Lyubov throw themselves into each other's arms, sobbing in despair for the loss of their orchard, their childhood, their happiness; they then leave, locking the door behind them. The spectator's identification with Gaev and Lyubov shifts markedly as the old servant, Firs, finding himself abandoned in the house, tries to open the locked door. This jolts the spectator into a more distanced perspective: the characters the audience so recently empathized with can no longer be viewed so sympathetically. With the abrupt shift to high distance, we experience the sudden and disturbing realization that the characters we grieved for are insensitive, and we reexamine their actions (and our own previous emotions) in the light of dramatic irony.

6

Distance: An Awareness of Fiction

In his rigorously analytical *Art and Imagination,* Roger Scruton concludes that the perception of art works is not the same as that accorded to ordinary objects of attention:[1] "My experience of a work of art involves a distinctive order of intentionality, derived from imagination and divorced from belief and judgement" (p. 77). When describing the aesthetic response, Scruton emphasizes the need to distinguish between cognitive states of mind, such as belief, and noncognitive states, such as imagining (p. 83). When we imagine, we are apparently indifferent to truth: the "content of our thought is the content of a belief; but the thought process itself is independent of this belief" (p. 89). Like Sartre, Scruton argues that imagining is subject to the will (p. 94) and that it "involves thought which is unasserted, and hence which goes beyond what is believed" (p. 97); imagining is a special case of "thinking of x as y" (p. 98). In Scruton's view, the nonliteral form of seeing that is "seeing as" does not refer to a species of judgment; what one "sees as" one sees without believing it to be there (p. 107). "Seeing as," therefore, is subject to the will (p. 109); it is an unasserted proposition that "goes beyond what is believed or inwardly asserted, and beyond what is strictly given in perception" (p. 112).

> The relation between "seeing as" and perception mirrors the relation between imagination and belief. "Seeing as" is like an "unasserted" visual experience: it is the embodiment of a thought which, if "asserted," would amount to a genuine perception, just as imagination, if "asserted," amounts to genuine belief. (p. 120)

Like Sartre, who maintains that perception is involuntary, Scruton contends that in ordinary sensory experience there is an unbidden belief in the existence of the object and the perception of the object is conditioned by that belief. Therefore such perception is not subject to the will (p. 114). Free imagination, that is, "seeing as," does not rest on belief in the existence of an object, and is therefore voluntary. The perceiver, permitting himself to see x as y, goes beyond belief, rational assertions, and "what is strictly given in perception." The aesthetic response rests on the imagination and is divorced from belief because the aesthetic object (the "object" of aesthetic perception) is nonexistent. Aesthetic emotions, then, are not founded on belief but on the entertainment of unasserted propositions (p. 128). The intensity of the aesthetic emotion "is a function not of the assertedness of its core of thought, but rather of the degree of 'imaginative involvement' that is experienced" (p. 130).

Scruton's argument is an appropriate one with which to begin the concluding chapter of this study. His book brings together many of the issues addressed in the previous chapters. Though it is not his intention to do so, nor does he employ the term, Scruton's analysis of art and imagination speaks to many of the same concerns as the foregoing discussions of distance. Scruton maintains that the aesthetic response to works of art requires a tacit lack of belief in the imagined object, *seeing* the art object *as* a nonexistent object (or fictional universe) and a voluntary use of the mind for that purpose. The element in the mental act of imagination which is tacitly aware of itself as voluntarily "seeing as," is the underlying premise of all the theories of distance that have been examined.

Though their concepts of distance have somewhat different parameters, for Bullough, Sartre, Metz, and Artaud, distance is a psychological phenomenon basic to the perception of art. Whereas Bullough sees distance as a general aesthetic principle, intrinsic to all art forms, Bertolt Brecht—in all but his latest writings—conceives of distance as unique to his specific kind of theatre, Epic Theatre. He argues in his early statements that traditional western ("aristotelian") drama lacks the element of distance altogether. Though Metz would agree with Bullough that all art forms require distance in order to combine aspects of the real and the unreal, he insists on the superiority of film due to *its* uniquely inherent level of distance. And while Artaud does not admit that his Theatre of Cruelty is premised on a concept of distance, he admits distance when he explains that the spectator is psychologically protected by his knowledge that his life is not in danger in the theatre, a protection which allows the most violent acts to significantly affect the viewer. For Artaud the theatre is a protected environment where one can permit himself to be vulnerable only because one knows he is safe. Like Bazin, Artaud assumes the operation of distance even as he, like Grotowski, explicitly advocates its elimination.

The only theorist examined for this book who seems really to reject any form of distance as a necessary condition for his work is Grotowski. Though initially premising his theories on a use of distance, in the latter part of his career, Grotowski moves beyond distance, and therefore theatre, when he does away with "audience," "actors," and "performance," seeking to create something akin to religious transformation, psychotherapy, or significant social encounters. No longer wanting any kind of psychological or emotional protection for the participants, Growtoski wants *actual* belief in the events. No longer a fictional event, the experience becomes a scene in the real lives of the participants. There is no longer a theatrical production on the "outside " of the viewer, but a religious ritual that immediately includes all the human beings present.

Grotowski himself agrees that he is no longer concerned with theatre or with art, and therefore, in fact, he does not disagree that distance is a necessary condition for art. Because his participants enter into his nontheatrical communal act, it is apparent that the whole issue of distance in relation to the event is no longer applicable.

If distance is intrinsic to the art experience, the question is how the phenomenon affects the perception of theatrical art. Bullough, Sartre, and Metz stress that distance allows for identification and empathy with fictional characters and the unreal world of the play.[2] Bullough argues that one result of "psychical" distance is the possibility for an emotional engagement with an object outside ourselves that is created by the projection of our own emotions onto the object. We experience emotions which seem "objectified" because they are placed in an object outside ourselves, hence removed from a practical response. Because they are pseudo-vicarious emotions (only *seemingly* the emotions of another person) we do not have to acknowledge our ownership of them, but, because we do own them, we permit ourselves to feel them more powerfully.

Sartre also maintains that the spectator's imaginative involvement in the unreal fictional world of the play causes him, on the one hand, to be psychologically protected, and, on the other, to be powerfully drawn to the imagined feelings of the character.[3] Sartre deepens the analysis of emotional projection: the emotions are literally "owned" by the spectator and therefore so are the qualities that are conferred upon the object. The spectators come to realize, at least tacitly, that the characters they are imagining embody aspects of themselves. Distance permits the involvement in the first instance and then is the condition for its development.

In Sartre's view, because consciousness has shifted to imaging ("seeing as," as Wittgenstein and Scruton term it),[4] it projects itself and its emotions into the image, and emotion carries with it belief. Scruton calls this state that of the "unasserted proposition," suggesting that virtual belief results not only from emotional but also from a rational frame of mind. This is appealing, but Scruton's analysis here seems excessively rationalistic. The projection of self into the image seems fundamentally an emotional investment, with other more rational responses following in consequence. Sartre argues that consciousness only becomes explicitly aware of its emotion when attempting to analyze its responses from an external perspective, that is, not from the inside of its own emotional response, but when projected on something outside—seeing its response in terms of objects, relationships, and explanations beyond itself.[5] Though emotion is by nature unreflective, a reflective consciousness can always direct itself upon emotion,[6] but this reflection requires special motivations. This is, of course, precisely the condition created by art, especially as understood in terms of its basis in distance.

The externally motivated consciousness of consciousness was what Brecht sought to achieve: to use the object to stimulate a reflective awareness of emotion. Though in his earliest writings he seems to have wanted to do away with the "magical" emotions of the theatre entirely, Brecht later came to the view that he wanted to create an awareness in the spectator of the characters' emotions and of the spectator's own emotions in response to the events onstage. Though Brecht believed that he could stimulate this critical reflection on one's emotions by means of alienation techniques alone, as was pointed out in the earlier discussion of Brecht's theories, an increased awareness of the mechanics of theatre, its conventions, does not in itself necessarily create a critical attitude. The employment of conventions does not increase awareness of them when they are accepted, and, as Susan Sontag points out, even the most radical of techniques can quickly become accepted conventions. The technique of exposing conventions can merely surprise the spectator into recognizing the convention, with no particular political import. In Brecht's theatre it is not only the techniques but also the subject matter invested in them that raises a political consciousness of a certain kind. The "larger perspective," which Bullough says is characteristic of all successful art, becomes political in the work of Brecht or George Bernard Shaw or Arthur Miller when it results from a particular style/content that encourages that point of view. *Mother Courage* and *Oedipus* may use the same technique of temporal remoteness, but the "larger perspectives" produced by each differ greatly.

Not only do distancing techniques alone, if they could be separated from content, lack thematic significance, it is also probably true that there is no such thing as a "distancing technique" isolated from a general stylistic context. Distance is a relational and relative factor, and no technique has absolute distancing value. For instance, having the actor directly address the audience does not necessarily increase distance, as when the Chorus of *Henry V* explicitly draws attention to the limitations of the stage, or when the Restoration actor turns to the audience with an aside expressing a very different attitude from that of his character. The actual effects of theatrical devices must always be understood within the context of the particular play and production: style, subject matter, and audience assumptions[7] are inseparably interrelated. We can certainly observe, and understand, the operation of distinct principles (such as distance) in art, but a work of art remains more analogous to an organic than to a mechanical entity; therefore the perception of every particular element in a work affects and is affected by the perception of every other. This point is of more than academic or theoretical significance, for we have seen in this study that claims are made for particular techniques or particular media independent of their contexts of style, subjects, and expectations.

It is tempting to reduce the variables in one's consideration of distance, especially for the active practitioner or critic, because the range of intellectual and emotional effects of distance seems so confoundingly infinite and so confusingly varied as to defy the comprehension of underlying principles. For this reason it is crucial to distinguish the variable components of the source of distance from the varying effects of distance in particular contexts.

From the analysis of the theorists in the previous chapters, it has become quite clear that the common thread in the theories of Bullough, Sartre, Brecht, and Metz (and, indeed, in the tradition that preceded them) is the emphasis on an awareness of fiction, a willingness to "see as." The spectator's awareness of fiction has long been recognized, if only implicitly, as an essential condition of the theatrical experience. Samuel Johnson, in his "Preface to Shakespeare," first made the argument, now famous, that images in the theatre are recognized for what they are.

> The drama exhibits successive imitations of successive actions; and why may not the second imitation represent an action that happened years after the first, if it be so connected with it, that nothing but time can be supposed to intervene? Time is, of all modes of existence, most obsequious to the imagination; a lapse of years is as easily conceived as a passage of hours. In contemplation we easily contract the time of real actions, and therefore willingly permit it to be contracted when we only see their imitation.
>
> It will be asked, how the drama moves, if it is not credited. It is credited with all the credit due to a drama. It is credited, whenever it moves, as a just picture of a real original; as representing to the auditor what he would himself feel.[8]

And with a similar vocabulary and a parallel argument, Coleridge claims that we take pleasure from such theatrical images because they are *not* reality.

> If we want to witness mere pain, we can visit the hospitals: if we seek the exhibition of mere pleasure, we can find it in ballrooms. It is the representation of it, not the reality, that we require, the imitation, and not the thing itself; and we pronounce it good or bad in proportion as the representation is an incorrect, or a correct imitation. The true pleasure we derive from theatrical performances arises from the fact that they are unreal and fictitious. If dying agonies were unfeigned, who, in these days of civilisation, could derive gratification from beholding them?[9]

The spectator's awareness that the theatrical event is a fiction fundamentally determines the viewer's experience.

An awareness of fiction is the most basic principle of distance in which there appears to be three distinguishable but interrelated components: 1) tacit knowing; 2) volition; and 3) perception *as* unreal.

It is that tacit awareness[10] of the fictionality of the images that provides the psychological protection that Bullough, Sartre, Artaud and Metz refer to. Indeed, this double perception of the reality of the medium and the fictionality of the image is the common basis for virtually all theorists writing on the phenomenon of the art experience.[11] Arthur Koestler argues that there exist two planes of mental activity: the spectator knows in one part of his mind that the people onstage are actors; yet in another part he experiences hope, fear, and pity, all of which are induced by events the viewer knows to be make-believe.[12] In Koestler's view, "the distinction between fact and fiction is a late acquisition of rational thought—unknown to the unconscious, and largely ignored by the emotions."[13]

The sometimes merely tacit awareness of this distinction between reality and fiction, however, is not actually lost upon the unconscious, or the emotions, as Koestler suggests. It is precisely because the viewer remains tacitly aware that the theatrical production is fiction that he or she can experience emotions without danger. The player of this "serious game" is permitted to experience a wider range of thoughts and emotions, with greater intensity and with greater rapidity than real life or sanity otherwise permit. With a psychoanalytic vocabulary and theoretical system, Norman Holland expresses a similar point of view, maintaining that the protection from our tacit awareness of fiction allows for more intense emotions:

> Our emotions in the literary situation seem stronger than in everyday life.... Within the literary "as if," because consciously we know we need only fantasy in response, we sink down to deeper levels of our mind. The aesthetic stance inhibits our motor activity; it therefore engages our moral and intellectual selves, not in suppressing or judging our deeper feelings, but in accepting and transforming them. Our "rind" of higher ego-functions, our "core" of deeply regressed ego—these make up a richer, longer kind of self than our ordinary one.[14]

In addition to tacit knowing or awareness, the second component of distance is volition. To be aware that the image is unreal, and yet to treat it with all the seriousness with which our minds are capable, requires complicity. Perhaps the most important contribution that Sartre makes to the understanding of distance lies in his insistence on the freedom of imagination as a voluntary act of consciousness. What one is free to do, one must will to do, and the element of volition is clearly implicit in both Bullough's and Brecht's concepts of distance.[15] Sartre most explicitly emphasizes the role of freedom, maintaining that one must will to initiate and sustain the imaginative act of consciousness.

Sartre's notions of the freedom of the imagination are quite important, but the significant matter here is not freedom *in* imagination—certainly not in the absolute sense he suggests—but his discussion of the freedom *to* imagine: that it is an inherently free act of will. If the key to distance is fictionality, it rests on the prior condition of a *willingness* to engage ourselves with an unreality. We cannot will to accept or reject what we believe to be real, we can only become inattentive toward it. But if engagement with fiction is not willed, then there is *nothing* of value (merely discomfort). The basis for distance is that we choose to act mentally toward an acknowledged unreality in some crucial ways as if it were reality. That we are free not to do so but that we choose to do so implicates us in its creation; it is a voluntary commitment to participate in the creation of an alternate universe. Because our response is voluntary, our relationship with the object is a highly personal one: our freedom to imagine (or not to imagine) invests our experience with the personal intensity characteristic of an investment of will.

The volitional aspect of distance implies that the perceiver is tacitly aware (and vice-versa); but neither consciousness nor will can exist without an object, even if the object is, as Sartre calls it, an "absence." The third component of distance is perception *as* unreal: that the *art work* is making unasserted propositions and that *we* are responding with a kind of simulated belief. It is here that the theories of Scruton, Sartre, and Bullough (as well as Samuel Johnson and Coleridge) most directly explain an aspect of the complex phenomenon of distance. With our tacit awareness of the art work as fictional, and our willingness to imaginatively engage, our consciousness is free from a reality criterion: we do not believe in the existence of the image, knowing the fictional world to be unreal. Therefore the art work, as Scruton explains, paradoxically makes "unasserted propositions" (or, as Philip Sidney says in *An Apology for Poetry,* "poetry asserteth not, therefore does not lie"). We do not judge the literal truth of the events because our imaginative experience is divorced from belief. In Sartre's terms, imaging is free from the constraints of the world.

Each of these components is implicated with and supports each of the others. Because we do not literally believe in the existence of the fictional world, it is our choice that we respond with conditional ("if . . . then") belief. Our conditional belief rests on a tacit awareness of fictionality, and our willingness to imaginatively engage it permits the projection of emotions onto the fictional object. The phenomenon of distance involves a double-edged psychic tension: because we know, as Johnson and Coleridge emphasize, that the work is fictional, we do not literally believe in the events onstage; but our willingness to imagine with the theatrical representation commits us to a metaphorical mode of thinking, a "seeing as"; the tacit awareness of this fiction and the conditional (and withdrawable) belief in the image provide the psychological protection that permits an intense projection of emotions, reinforcing our simulated belief in the image. Because our belief is conditional, based on our own willingness to imagine and our recognition of the image as unreality, it is "owned" by our minds. As Roman Ingarden explains, the unreal aesthetic object exists in the mind of the perceiver, resulting from his or her concretization of the actual, indeterminate art object.[16]

This role of the spectator in the creation of the fictional universe explains Johnson's statement that the drama "is credited with all the credit due to a drama." He is right when he insists that we are never deluded in the theatre, and because we choose to imaginatively engage and are not restricted by a reality criterion, the unities of time and place are inessential: if we can metaphorically see the actors "as if" they are characters, then we can imagine, even in the short span of two to three hours (or two to three seconds), those characters in various fictional places and in various fictional times. The mental capacity to metaphorically engage "the fog comes on little cat feet" has no *inherent* difficulty with engaging Athens at one side of a stage and Rome at another; the difficulty is only conventional.

The phenomenon of distance also explains Coleridge's notion of "the true pleasure we derive from theatrical performance." Even if the drama presents "dying agonies," we take pleasure because we know, on some level of our consciousness, that the event is not real, and because we experience the freedom of our own imagination, and, no doubt, on condition that it will produce a "larger perspective." We choose to imagine the nonexistent fictional world, and there is pleasure in our freedom to respond. In addition, because our imagination is not limited by the constraints of the real world, we take pleasure in its flights of fancy. It is for this reason that, as Scruton says, the intensity of our aesthetic emotion is not a function of "its core of thought, but rather of the degree of 'imaginative involvement' that is experienced." The intensity of our imaginative engagement determines our pleasure. Our tacit awareness of fiction and our willingness to "perceive metaphorically," allow us to participate in the creation of a satisfying imaginative order.

It might be objected that the conclusions I have come to merely make distance another term for the imagination, or for a particular species of imagination. The latter may indeed be an accurate description of distance. As a component of ordinary reality-perception, distance is not equivalent to all forms of imagination. Moreover, if a distinction can be made between the creative and the responsive imaginations, clearly distance would be concerned with the latter. In a sense self-consciousness, knowing that one is "seeing as," is the single unique feature of distance, but in isolating this single component, it is important to stress the interdependence of awareness, volition and unreality in this self-aware "seeing as." "Awareness of fiction" formulates the concept of distance in a useful way but only when its implications are understood. It should also be noted, as something clearly implicit in this concept, that distance is neither simply an on/off condition nor exclusively one of degrees but both: self-awareness, for instance, either exists or does not, but the self-awareness may be induced to a greater or lesser degree.

In addition to the effects of the contexts previously referred to, another great cause for the variability of distancing effects is the variability of the three constituent elements. Because they are interactive, an increase or decrease in one element influences the others. For instance, a loss of connection with reality by the fiction (e.g., incredible motivations) taxes our willingness to "go along with it" and may increase our awareness of fictionality excessively; or, to reverse the direction of the mental experiment, depriving the spectator of his freedom (as occurs in some happenings) creates a condition of reality for the spectator (*his* reality vis-a-vis the tyranny of the actors) and loss of consciousness of any fiction. As Bullough noted, the phenomenon of distance exists between the two extremes. Perhaps the only "rule" for this is the maintenance of some degree of psychic tension between an awareness of the image as a fictional object and of the real object that is its generator. It is an interesting phenomenon, well known in the theatre, that an excessive realism— such as an actor being whipped in "too real" a fashion, or a "too real" head of Macbeth hung on a pike—will destroy what is usually called "the illusion of reality."[17] Perhaps the more accurate statement is that when an element is perceived as only real, it is therefore no longer perceived metaphorically.

In the spectrum of psychological distance, a sudden increase in distance may produce an increased awareness of fiction (theatre *as* theatre), an increased awareness of the "larger perspective" which relates the play to society, philosophy, etc., an increased consciousness of emotion (reflection on one's previous emotion) and perhaps even a critical examination of that emotion, increased awareness of the play's internal structure, or all of these at once.

Decreasing the viewer's awareness of fiction may produce a more intense involvement in the fictional world and engagement with its "reality," a more intense identification with the characters and involvement in their "inner lives," greater empathy (projection of one's own emotional life into the character-images), a climax of the emotional experience, or all of these at once.

The actual "limits" of distance are most clearly revealed by Grotowski, on the one hand, and Brecht on the other. Grotowski initially wanted to take theatre as far as it could go, to reduce distance to the extent that the theatrical event would become a "direct" confrontation. When the confrontation could not be as direct and without pretense as he wished, Grotowski eventually moved beyond the limits of theatre; he eliminated the element of unreality from his work, creating instead religious, ritualistic ceremonies. Obviously, the abandonment of theatre made distance unnecessary, but it is relevent to note that it appears to have been precisely the phenomenon of distance itself that frustrated Grotowski—the fictionality, the self-consciousness, and the requirement for freedom that made his actors' demands on the spectators seem tyranny.

Brecht pushed distance in the other direction: sometimes his theories demand *only* the perception of the idea, thereby using distancing techniques to exceed the limits of aesthetic distance. No longer aware of the actor as character, but as an attitude or an idea, the spectator in the Epic Theatre is often encouraged to become aware of only an abstract concept without even the grounding of a vivid dramatic image. When Brecht is more interested in the spectator's recognition of a principle (than any kind of imaginative involvement), he sometimes draws attention to the real *as* real, thereby excluding the fusion of real object and unreal aesthetic image.

While both Brecht's and Artaud's ideas tested the limits of distance in different directions, neither abandoned art (unlike Grotowski). But they, and to an even greater extent their followers, make exclusive claims on theatre in terms of distance. Where Brecht assumes that traditional ("Aristotelian") theatre excludes all distance, describing it as irrational, hypnotic, a waking dream, Artaud gladly embraces those terms but says that traditional ("Western") theatre is over-distanced, rationalistic, verbalistic. The theorists who are less committed to a particular notion of theatre seem to agree that some degree of distance is a necessary condition of theatrical art but that an excessive awareness of its fictionality is as dangerous to imaginative participation as is too little awareness, which endangers volition.

Neither of the exclusive claims for what are sometimes called the illusionistic and the nonillusionistic theatres is correct, therefore. In fact, Brecht and Artaud can be best understood as stressing different parts of a continuous spectrum rather than different conceptions of theatre. This would help to explain how it is that the theories of Brecht and Artaud, so often taken to be antithetical, may be seen to be equally valid in the same modern works, such as Peter Brook's production of *The Marat / Sade.* In any case it seems clear that Brecht made a selective use of empathy—identification with the feelings and point of view of characters—in his later plays (for example, Katrin in *Mother Courage,* Grusha and Azdak in *Caucasian Chalk Circle,* Shen Te in *Good Woman of Setzuan*), as an instrument of his purpose. If it is true, as Brecht says, that empathy is not required in order to produce emotion, it seems also to be true that distance—as the general condition of a work—does not preclude the use of empathy.

It is exactly in terms of this tension between two extremes, total empathy on the one hand and its complete elimination on the other, that Bullough's essay, and its significance, can best be understood. Distance, formulated in Bullough's essay as the aesthetic tension between these two extremes, is the basis of a general aesthetic principle: distance is fundamental to the aesthetic consciousness and is variable. The spectrum of psychological distance allows various degrees of a personal relationship with the art object, on the one hand, and an awareness of unreality on the other. As Bullough explains, "Distance represents in aesthetic appreciation ... a quality inherent in the impersonal, yet *so* intensely personal, relation which the human being entertains with art" (p. 117).

The deliberate manipulation of distance is one of the distinctive features of twentieth-century theatre and may be the result of the various theatrical experiments since the beginning of the century. When it is seen that the avant-garde movements produced few plays of lasting value and no permanently useful forms, it may seem that they failed in every way except to develop techniques that were used by less adventuresome playwrights. This study of distance, however, suggests another point of view. Perhaps the major contribution of experimentalists such as Jarry, Hauptmann, Maeterlinck, the Dadaists, Cocteau, Kaiser, etc. was the raising of the consciousness of theatre artists to the phenomenon of distance. The fixed genres that dominated the theatre up until that time tended also to fix distance. Though the phenomenon of distance existed prior to the twentieth century, the deliberate and conscious manipulation of it by theatre practitioners seems to be a recent development.

While it was surely inadvertent, a result of the experimentation with techniques of both extreme naturalism and extreme expressionism seems to have been the discovery of a deeper principle, which is proving more revolutionary than any that was intended—and which has so taken over theatrical art that it goes virtually unnoticed. The dramatist today chooses a theatrical style, and therefore a general distance norm, for his or her play, just as he or she chooses characters and situations. Moreover, not only have the fixed canons of genre fallen in the theatre, so have the fixed canons of style: distance is manipulated from one moment to the next in a play, inducing empathy and then objectivity and then again empathy. The plays of Harold Pinter or Edward Bond defy description in traditional genre or style terms; they must be understood, I believe, in terms of style shifts at the service of the manipulation of distance.

The deliberate manipulation of distance is, to a great extent, the underlying factor that determines theatrical style in this century: degrees of stylization may alter from one work to another according to the specific strategies of the works; and degrees of distance alter from one moment to the next within any individual play.[18] While both of these principles can be illustrated in the plays of Shakespeare,[19] they are easier to illustrate in contemporary works. Two plays that have been powerfully effective in the modern theatre, *The Death of A Salesman*, by Arthur Miller, and *Mother Courage*, by Bertolt Brecht, have similar social themes though Miller uses the metaphor of salesmanship to explore the environment of economic competition, and Brecht's Thirty Years' War is a metaphor for competitive survival. Yet the plays "look" strikingly different because Brecht maintains a relatively high degree of distance as the normative basis for his play while Miller maintains a relatively low degree of distance. Brecht invites us to stand back and recognize the strangeness of familiar human behavior, while Miller invites us to get close to the characters and recognize the familiarity of strange human behavior. Brecht must first establish remoteness, Miller closeness. What is important, however, is that both plays can only be effective if the general level of distance that is established is reversed at a climactic point: in *Mother Courage*, distance is significantly reduced with the strong exploitation of empathy for Katrin when she has climbed on the wagon to beat a drum to warn the town (though she knows that she will be shot for doing it); in *Salesman,* distance is increased when Willy "consults" with his memory/fantasy brother who advises him to convert his life into cash for his sons. These reversals succeed because they have been prepared for earlier by more minor distance reversals: the more notable of these preparatory reversals in *Mother Courage* is Mother Courage's silent scream at the end of the third scene; one of the more extended instances of a preparatory reversal in *Salesman* is Willy's fantasy in the restaurant bathroom.

I do not mean to suggest that the deliberate manipulation of distance is the only characteristic of modern drama or that it is the only underlying principle at work, but it does seem to be of great and pervasive significance and to run at a deeper level through the drama of this century than the stylistic fashions associated with particular decades or playwrights. Bullough's essay was written at a time when European drama had been undergoing a kind of competition among aesthetic points of view, not only a competition between traditionalists and modernists, but just as much between various traditionalists and various modernists. I think that without quite understanding it Bullough had perceived in that new turbulence a thread that was to be the mark of the drama of this century.

The heady freedom that all this implies for the artist, and the responsibility for making choices that this thrusts upon him, means a new level of awareness for the spectator, as well. If a play is not tragedy merely because it is in that or any other genre, then the play is what it is because its form itself is significant, and therefore the spectator is required to comprehend the work not only *within* its form (and in comparison with plays with similar forms) but also as a form created out of the needs of that work. A new level of self-consciousness both for the artist and the spectator is required. This heightened self-consciousness is central to Bullough's insight. Even if aesthetic distance is an essential characteristic of art, as Bullough argues, it is also true that there were particular reasons why this would become clear in the twentieth century and have special relevance to the dramatic art of this century.

Only rarely in the work of pre-Romantic playwrights (most notably Euripides, Shakespeare and Molière) have sharply contrasting distance states been exploited consciously and strategically with noncomic drama: Euripides' *Orestes,* and Shakespeare's *Troilus and Cressida,* and Molière's *Tartuffe,* for instance, have posed particular difficulties for critics who attempted to place them in traditional categories. "Romantic irony," described as the perceiver's consciousness of the artist's detachment from his work, seems to be the first critical term invented to recognize the manipulation of distance in a serious work (e.g., Don Juan bids a tender farewell to Spain and his beloved, vows to think only of her, and promptly grows green and nauseated by sea sickness).

Today it is rare to find a play with serious ambitions that does *not* exploit sharp alterations in distance, though it seems that this has not been generally observed by critics. For this reason I believe that some critical consciousness-raising of the role of distance in modern drama is long overdue. Indeed, even this study of the phenomenon of aesthetic distance, though hardly exhaustive, is long overdue. Since Bullough's highly influential article the concept has been accepted or rejected in citations or in footnotes, with little attempt to make sustained arguments. The concept is too important and has too much explanatory power to be refuted by quibbles with Bullough's language. The concept itself, or elements of it, long predates Bullough, and since his article early in this century, the concept of distance has been independently reformulated by artists, critics, and aestheticians. While the study which concludes here is not adequate for a full understanding of the aesthetic phenomenon, I hope that it has advanced our comprehension by clarifying issues and by pointing to the significance of the concept of distance to art theory.

Notes

Chapter 1

1. Though the eighteenth-century British thinkers forcefully articulate a concept of disinterestedness at some length, a similar notion is used as early as the fourth century B.C. in the works of Aristotle. Though Aristotle does not discuss the disinterested perception of art (without self-interest), he does distinguish disinterested arts, those not aiming at utility (therefore, without self-interest), from other types which do aim at such utility. Aristotle explains that "every art and every investigation, and likewise every practical pursuit or undertaking, seems to aim at some good: hence it has been well said that the Good is that at which all things aim. (It is true that a certain variety is to be observed among the ends at which the arts and sciences aim: in some cases the activity of practising the art is itself the end [such as flute-playing], whereas in others the end is some product over and above the mere exercise of the art [such as house-building]; and in the arts whose ends are certain things beside the practice of the arts themselves, these products are essentially superior in value to the activities.) (p. 3)... Works of art have their merit in themselves, so that it is enough if they are produced having a certain quality of their own." *Nicomachian Ethics,* trans. H. Rackham (New York: G.P. Putnam's Sons, 1934), p. 85.

   Also, Aristotle states that "[As arts multiplied], some were directed to the necessities in life, others to recreation, and the inventors of the latter were naturally always regarded as wiser than the inventors of the former, because their branches of knowledge did not aim at utility." *Metaphysics,* trans. W.D. Ross, 2d ed. (Oxford: Clarendon Press, 1928), 981b17.

2. See Shaftesbury's *Characteristics of Men, Manners, Opinions, Times,* etc., ed. John M. Robertson, 2 vols. (Gloucester, Mass.: Peter Smith, 1963), especially "Miscellany III."

3. Jerome Stolnitz, "Of the Origins of 'Aesthetic Disinterestedness,'" *The Journal of Aesthetics and Art Criticism* 20 (Winter 1961): 131-43.

4. Immanuel Kant, *The Critique of Judgement,* trans. James Creed Meredith (Oxford: Clarendon Press, 1952), pp. 48-49.

5. Ibid., p. 49.

6. Arthur Schopenhauer, *The World as Will and Idea,* trans. R.B. Haldane and John Kemp (New York: Humanities Press, 1964).

7. *Laughter: An Essay on the Meaning of the Comic,* trans. Cloudesley Brereton and Fred Rothwell (New York: Macmillan, 1924).

8. Samuel Taylor Coleridge, *Biographia Literaria,* ed. J. Shawcross, vol. 2 (London: Oxford University Press, 1907), pp. 49-50.

9. *The Genealogy of Morals, Peoples and Countries,* trans. H.B. Samuel in *The Complete Works of Friedrich Nietzsche,* ed. Oscar Levy, vol. 13 (London: George Allen and Unwin, 1910), p. 131.

10. The notion of distance has broader origins than Bullough's specific formulations. The word "distance" has long had a usage in English to suggest emotional withdrawal or noninvolvement, as Shakespeare uses it in *The Lover's Complaint:* "She kept... cold distance" (lines 236-37). Distance as a metaphor already had an appropriate resonance for the speaker of English.

    In 1808 Schlegel implied a similar meaning of emotional withdrawal when he said: "In France the young men of quality who sat on the stage lay in wait to discover something to laugh at;... all theatrical effect requires a certain distance, and when viewed too closely appears ludicrous." See August Wilhelm von Schlegel, *Course of Lectures on Dramatic Art and Literature,* trans. John Black (London: Henry G. Bohn, 1846), p. 256.

11. Edward Bullough, "'Psychical Distance' as a Factor in Art and an Aesthetic Principle," *British Journal of Psychology* 5 (June 1912): 91. Subsequent references to this esssay will appear in parentheses in the text throughout the rest of the chapter.

12. Kant, *The Critique of Judgement,* p. 62.

13. The phenomenon but not the concept of "distance" was also observed by Aristotle: "Objects which in themselves we view with pain, we delight to contemplate when reproduced with minute fidelity: such as the forms of the most ignoble animals and of dead bodies." See *Aristotle's Theory of Poetry and Fine Art,* trans. S.H. Butcher, 4th ed. (London: Macmillan and Co., 1922), p. 15.

14. Difficult to defend are those theories which maintain that aesthetic perception is totally dependent on appearance. Such is Vincent Tomas's view as expressed in his essay, "Aesthetic Vision," in *Philosophical Review* 68 (1959): 52-67. Tomas's major distinction, which he uses to differentiate aesthetic and nonaesthetic perception, is between "stimulus objects" and "appearances." Tomas maintains that in nonaesthetic perception, "our attention is directed toward the stimulus objects that appear to us... and we do not primarily notice the ways in which these objects appear.... When we see things aesthetically, our attention is directed toward appearances and we do not particularly notice the thing that presents the appearance" (p. 53). Frank Sibley in "Aesthetics and the Looks of Things" (*The Journal of Philosophy* 56 [November 1959]: 905-15) makes a similar claim when he contends that aesthetic perception requires attention to appearances and also to the real looks of things.

    I find it very difficult to defend a view that distinguishes perceptual experiences by contending that aesthetic experiences focus on "appearances" or "surface qualities" while nonaesthetic do not. Surely we can quite easily argue that "appearances" are often quite important when we practically perceive; we have to see the engine of our TR3 via "appearances" if we are going to go about fixing it. Tomas's and Sibley's theories provide a specious and confusing distinction.

15. One of the most prominent advocates of the "aesthetic attitude" is Jerome Stolnitz. Although Stolnitz does not argue, as Bullough does, that we have a separate psychological force that determines our aesthetic perception of art works, he does believe that we adopt a special disinterested attitude when perceiving art. For Stolnitz, our attitude determines our perceptual experience of the world. The aesthetic attitude "'isolates' the object and focuses upon it.... Hence the object is not seen in a fragmentary or passing manner, as it is in 'practical' perception.... Its whole nature and character are dwelt upon." *Aesthetics and Philosophy of Art Criticism* (Boston: Houghton Mufflin Co., 1960), p. 35. For a complete listing of Stolnitz's works on the "aesthetic attiude," see the bibliography.

George Dickie objects that such a distinction between modes of perception—aesthetic perception versus practical perception—can be made, claiming that what appears to be a perceptual distinction—how we perceive theatrical events versus how we view everyday objects—is only a motivational or intentional one, distinguishing between different purposes behind the perceiving. According to Dickie, "a person's motive or intention is different from his action": there is only *one* way to perceive a work of art, although the listener or viewer "may be more or less attentive and there may be a variety of motives, intentions, and reasons for doing so and a variety of ways of being distracted" from the object. "The Myth of the Aesthetic Attitude," *American Philosophical Quarterly* 1 (January 1964); reprinted in *Introductory Readings in Aesthetics*, ed. John Hospers (New York: The Free Press, 1969), pp. 28-44.

But Dickie's view seems enormously reductive, because a person can be both quite attentive to a theatrical performance of *Three Sisters* and to an everyday discussion with his or her family in the living room, yet somehow the two experiences—perceptually and imaginatively—seem *qualitatively* different. Even if only motives were considered—which Dickie permits—it is difficult to understand how any reasonably complex concept of perception would not have to account for the difference in the quality of attention directed toward a real lion and that toward a painting of a lion. Dickie's objection concerning the perceptual distinction does not seriously refute the fundamental distinction made by Bullough: that a notable difference exists between the perceiving during the aesthetic experience and otherwise.

This notion of "attention" to the art object is most fully developed by Eliseo Vivas, who characterizes the aesthetic experience as "rapt attention that involves the intransitive apprehension of an object's immanent meanings." For Vivas, the response is "disinterested"—blocking out personal beliefs and values—during the time it takes place. See "A Definition of the Esthetic Experience," *The Journal of Philosophy* 34 (November 1937): 628-34; and *The Artistic Transaction* (Columbus, Ohio: Ohio State University Press, 1963).

Focusing one's attention is also stressed by Curt John Ducasse, who claims that with aesthetic contemplation, "the attention is withdrawn from everything other than the object of aesthetic contemplation, and inwardly the ground is cleared for the reception of feeling of that object." See "The Aesthetic Attitude," Chapter 9, *The Philosophy of Art* (New York: The Dial Press, 1929).

The psychologist who has forcefully stressed the role of selective attention in his discussions of perception is William James, who maintains that experience is what we agree to attend to. "Only those things which I *notice* shape my mind—without selective interest, experience is an utter chaos" (p. 402). For James, attention is the "focalization, concentration of consciousness" and "implies withdrawal from some things in order to deal effectively with others." *The Principles of Psychology*, vol. 1 (New York: Henry Holt and Co., 1890), pp. 403-4.

16. Susanne Langer, *Philosophy in a New Key: A Study in the Symbolism of Reason, Rite, and Art*, 3rd ed. (Cambridge, Mass.: Harvard University Press, 1957).

17. Susanne Langer, *Feeling and Form: A Theory of Art* (New York: Charles Scribner's Sons, 1953), p. 319.

18. Some theorists *have* analyzed Bullough's essay, notably D.J. Crossley and Allan Casebier. Crossley describes Bullough's distance as a three-staged program for aesthetic awareness, but tends to interpret Bullough's notion of "block" as merely blocking action, a simplistic treatment of a more complex phenomenon (or phenomena) that Bullough has in mind. See "The Aesthetic Attitude: Back in Gear with Bullough," *The Personalist* 56 (Summer 1975): 336-45.

In an attempt to deal with some of the confusing aspects of Bullough's essay, Allan Casebier offers a more elaborate vocabulary for distance, claiming that there are two types of distance: "attentional distance" and "emotional distance." Attentional distance has to do with the degree to which the viewer is attending the object, and emotional distance with the function of the viewer's emotions in response to the object. For Casebier, there is no necessary connection between the two types of distance, and he argues that Bullough vacillates between the two notions in his discussion of distance.

As the analysis of the Bullough essay will hopefully make apparent, for Bullough, there *is* a connection between attentional and emotional distance, so much so that it is difficult to make such a distinction. This specious distinction reduces the complexity of Bullough's argument, and its subtlety. For Casebier's analysis, see "The Concept of Aesthetic Distance," *The Personalist* (Winter 1971): 70-91; reprinted in *Aesthetics: A Critical Anthology,* ed. George Dickie and Richard J. Sclafani (New York: St. Martin's Press, 1977), pp. 783-99.

19.   Although Dickie treats aesthetic attitude theories as merely weaker versions of Bullough's theory of distance (and hence Dickie's rejection of both within the same essay), and though the two concepts are related, Bullough tries to distinguish distance from disinterestedness (a lack of personal interest). And though Bullough maintains that the psychological phenomenon of distance allows for aesthetic experience, he by no means claims that aesthetic experience results from merely attending to the art work. Bullough's concern is not so much the attitude we bring to our perception of works of art, but rather the emotional, intellectual, and "personal" dimensions of our relationships to, and our experience of, that art work. And though Bullough postulates that distance is an "essential characteristic" of the "aesthetic consciousness"—"that special mental attitude towards . . . various forms of Art," his theory deals with how that ingredient affects, determines, and creates our experience of art. Whereas the aesthetic attitude theories are primarily concerned with a disinterested frame of reference that the spectator brings to the work of art, Bullough's theory specifically addresses the "objective" investment of emotions in the art work, as well as the "personal relation" to the art work. Although not always clear, explicit, or complete in his explanations, Bullough is attempting to describe how this apparent component of the aesthetic consciousness—psychical distance—qualitatively affects our experience of art.

Although many aesthetic attitude theories are insightful and pertinent to some of the issues discussed in this book, I will more directly deal with, and limit my analysis to, theories of distance, allowing me to focus more sharply on the specific issues in an attempt to get at a clearer understanding of the ever-elusive concept of distance.

Chapter 2

1.   Jean-Paul Sartre, *The Psychology of Imagination* (New York: Philosophical Library, 1948), p. 36. Subsequent references to this book will appear in parentheses in the text throughout the rest of the chapter.

2.   Sartre, *Imagination,* trans. Forrest Williams (Ann Arbor: The University of Michigan Press, 1962), p. 143.

3.   Although Sartre uses the word "image," it is important to note that he does not conceive of the image as a mere "mental picture" or as a psychic content. To do so, according to Sartre, would be committing the "illusion of immanence": conceiving the image in terms of space, thereby constructing the world of the mind out of objects entirely like those of the external world (*Psychology of Imagination,* pp. 6-7). For Sartre, the image is not a "picture" but merely a relationship between object and consciousness, or, put yet another way, and *act* of consciousness.

4. Eugene F. Kaelin, *An Existentialist Aesthetic: The Theories of Sartre and Merleau-Ponty* (Madison: The University of Wisconsin Press, 1962), p. 65.

5. Sartre, "Myth and Reality in the Theatre," in *Tell Me Lies,* ed. Michael Kustow, Geoffrey Reeves, and Albert Hunt (Indianapolis: The Bobbs-Merrill Co., 1968), pp. 199-201.

6. Ibid.

7. Sartre, "Brecht and the Classics," in *Sartre on Theatre,* trans. Frank Jellinek, ed. Michel Contat and Michel Rybalka (New York: Pantheon Books, 1976), p. 56.

8. Sartre, *Saint Genet: Actor and Martyr,* trans. Bernard Frechtman (New York: George Braziller, Inc., 1963), pp. 392-93.

9. Sartre, *The Emotions: Outline of a Theory,* trans. Bernard Frechtman (New York: Philsophical Library, 1948), pp. 90-91.

10. Ibid., p. 73.

11. Because Sartre contends that a drop into emotion is not a rational response, and emotion causes the consciousness to respond to the world as if ruled by magic, the consciousness cannot critically analyze the emotion while actually experiencing it. Because consciousness on one level believes in its emotional state and projects its emotions onto the object outside of itself (even though we can say that the object stimulated such projection), the consciousness cannot critically reflect on that state of belief without approaching its response in a more rational manner. Consciousness only becomes explicitly aware of itself when attempting to analyze its own responses from a more external perspective, that is, not from the inside of its own emotional response, but from the outside—seeing its own response in terms of objects, relationships, and explanations beyond itself. Sartre claims that emotion is by nature unreflective (Ibid., pp. 50-51), and that usually actions in the world are carried out without leaving the unreflective plane, but he does maintain that a reflective consciousness can always direct itself upon emotion (p. 91), but this reflection requires special motivations.

12. Sartre, "On Dramatic Style," in *Sartre on Theatre,* p. 12.

13. Sartre, "Theatre and Cinema," in *Sartre on Theatre,* p. 62.

14. Ibid., pp. 62-63.

15. Sartre, "On Dramatic Style," p. 12.
     Perhaps it is Sartre's alignment with Brecht that causes confusion about his concept of distance, as when Timothy J. Reiss states that "what Sartre forces on us in the theatre" is that "we become conscious of being involved rather than simple onlookers." With Sartre's view of distance as imaginative involvement in the unreal, he would never agree that his goal is to achieve self-conscious awareness of one's own theatrical experience. See Reiss's "Psychical Distance and Theatrical Distancing in Sartre's Drama," *Yale French Studies,* 46 (1971): 13.

16. Interview on *The Condemned of Altona,* in *Sartre on Theatre,* p. 259.

17. Ibid., p. 256.
     Sartre's concern for the simultaneous creation of the production's temporal remoteness and the spectator's intense identification (almost to the point of "self annihilation") is described by C.R. Bukala: "The play . . . becomes a religious rite for Sartre and a certain reserve of manner, which, instead of increasing familiarity, rather increases the distance between characters and their dramatic activity and audience." "Sartre's Dramatic Philosophical Quest," *Thought* 48 (Spring 1973):87.

18. Sartre, "On Dramatic Style," p. 9.

19. Sartre, "Myth and Reality," p. 199.

20. Sartre describes this confusion in terms of a production about the Vietnam war: "What we see is neither real, because after all we are looking at actors acting, nor unreal, as everything that happens makes us aware of the reality of the war in Vietnam. And in spite of everything it is the reality that affects the spectator, because it is the noises, the colours, the movements which finally bring about a certain kind of trance or bewilderment, depending upon the individual. The public are not asked to take part in the performance: they are for the most part kept at a distance. They receive this mixture of broken sketches, interrupted at the moments where an illusion is about to be created, as a blow in the face. And at the end they find themselves before a real event, a real happening, even though this happening is renewed every evening" ("Myth and Reality," p. 200).

21. Ibid.

22. Samuel L. Bethell suggests this concept of "multi-consciousness" when explaining the audience experience of Shakespearean plays. Bethell maintains that in Shakespeare, the use of conventions and naturalism demand of the audience a dual mode of attention: dual awareness of the play world and the real world. Bethell contends that there is a "popular dramatic tradition" which consists of the audience's ability "to respond spontaneously and unconsciously on more than one plane of attention at the same time," calling this "the principle of multi-consciousness." See *Shakespeare and The Popular Tradition* (Westminster: Staples Press, 1944), p. 29.

23. Mary Warnock, *Imagination* (Berkeley: University of California, 1976), p. 174.

24. Ibid., p. 194.

25. Maurice Merleau-Ponty, *The Phenomenology of Perception*, trans. Colin Smith (New York: The Humanities Press, 1962), pp. 238-40.

26. Kaelin, *An Existentialist Aesthetic*, p. 364.

27. Ibid., pp. 162-63.

28. Bullough only implicitly refers to the voluntary aspect of distance whereas Sartre explicitly makes freedom a fundamental condition.

Chapter 3

1. *Brecht on Theatre*, ed. John Willett (New York: Hill and Wang, 1964), p. 9.

2. "Conversation with Bert Brecht," *Die Literarische Welt*, 1926, in *Brecht on Theatre*, p. 15.

3. The early phase of Brecht's career began in 1918 and lasted over ten years, until 1933 when Brecht left Germany and remained in exile until after World War II.

4. Brecht, "Short Description of a New Technique of Acting," *Versuche* II, 1951, in *Brecht on Theatre*, p. 145.

5. Various critics, failing to examine the evolution of Brecht's ideas, see his alienation techniques as opposing emotion altogether, or as being antithetical to the notion of "spectator involvement." Though his radical theoretical statements of the early years do suggest such an opposition, they give way in the later years to more sophisticated, balanced explanations. For a more complete understanding of how such confusions oversimplify Brecht's theories, see: W.A.J. Steer, "Brecht's Epic Theatre: Theory and Practice," *The*

Modern Langauge Review 63 (July 1968): 636-49; Charles C. Hampton, Jr., "Verfremdungseffekt," *Modern Drama* 14 (December 1971): 340-54; Donald S. Woodland, "The Danger of Empathy in *Mother Courage," Modern Drama* 15 (May 1972): 125-29; Claudio Vincentini, "Pirandello, Stanislavsky, Brecht, and the 'Opposition Principle,'" *Modern Drama* 20 (December 1977): 381-92; and Douglas Charles Wixson, Jr., "The Dramatic Techniques of Thorton Wilder and Bertolt Brecht," *Modern Drama* 15 (May 1972): 112-24.

For a discussion of how the concept of alienation has been misunderstood, see Edward Albee, "An Interview with Edward Albee," in *The American Theatre Today*, ed. Alan S. Downer (New York: Basic Books, 1967), pp. 111-23; and for additional critics who establish an opposition between alienation and spectator involvement, see Thomas B. Markus, "Tiny Alice and Tragic Catharsis," *Educational Theatre Journal* 17 (October 1965): 225-33; and Robert Wallace, "The Zoo Story: Albee's Attack on Fiction," *Modern Drama* 16 (June 1973): 45-54.

J.L. Styan, a dramatic theorist and critic who has been significantly influenced by Brecht in the formulation of his own theories, suggests an antithesis in his most recent book, *Drama, Stage and Audience* (London: Cambridge University Press, 1975), but an antithesis that does not seem to be Brecht's. Styan claims that increased distance in "non-illusory" theatre creates involvement by forcing the spectator to openly acknowledge the conventions of the theatre, recognizing that he or she is viewing a performance, whereas reduced distance in "illusory" theatre diminishes the spectator's mental participation because it creates an intense illusion in the spectator, allowing for a "belief" in the event. Although Styan's theoretical opposition resembles that of the other critics, it fundamentally differs in that, supposedly, an increase in distance increases involvement whereas a decrease in distance reduces it.

6.   "Notes to Die Rundköpfe und Die Spitzköpfe," *Gesammelte Werke,* vol. 2, 1938, in *Brecht on Theatre*, p. 101.

7.   In "A Short Organum for the Theatre," 1948, Brecht states: "Even if empathy, or self-identification with the character, can be usefully indulged in at rehearsals (something to be avoided in performance) it has to be treated just as one of a number of methods of observation. It helps when rehearsing, for even though the contemporary theatre has applied it in an indiscriminate way it has none the less led to subtle delineation of personality" (*Brecht on Theatre*, p. 195).

8.   Ibid., p. 191.

9.   "Notes on Erwin Strittmatter's Play *Katzgraben,*" *Junge Kunst,* 1958, in *Brecht on Theatre,* pp. 248-49.

10.   Brecht, "A Short Organum," p. 194.

11.   That the spectator's awareness of the event as theatre creates a more active mental participation, is central to J.L. Styan's thesis in *Drama, Stage and Audience.*

12.   Stephen Heath suggests that Epic Theatre involves "a refusal of separation" between audience and event, a repositioning of the spectator: "It is this fixed position of separation-representation-speculation... that Brecht's distanciation seeks to undermine. [Walter] Benjamin opens a discussion of epic theatre ... by describing a certain *refusal of separation* which it entails.... It is this breaking down of separation on which the establishment of distance depends, the repositioning-depositioning of the spectator in a critical-multi-perspective." "Lessons from Brecht," *Screen* 15 (Summer 1974):108-9.

13. All of Brecht's techniques are time-related concepts, that is, his ideas are constantly evolving through the years.

14. "A Short Organum," pp. 194-95.

15. Heath also suggests that distanciation involves "thinking within and without, in and beyond the play," creating a critical perspective. See "Lessons from Brecht," p. 115.

16. "Indirect Impact of the Epic Theatre," *Versuche* 7, 1933, in *Brecht on Theatre*, pp. 57-58.

17. "A Short Organum," p. 200.

18. Roland Barthes compares this highlighting of the "knots" separating each scene to the work of Diderot and Eisenstein: "The whole of Diderot's aesthetics rests on the identification of theatrical scene and pictorial tableau: the perfect play is a succession of tableaux, that is, a gallery, an exhibition.... The tableau ... is a pure cut-out segment with clearly defined edges.... The epic scene in Brecht, the shot in Eisenstein are so many tableaux; they are scenes which are *laid out* (in the sense in which one says *the table is laid*), which answer perfectly to that dramatic unity theorized by Diderot: firmly cut out..., erecting a meaning but manifesting the production of that meaning." "Diderot, Brecht, Eisenstein" in *Image—Music—Text*, trans. Stephen Heath (New York: Hill and Wang, 1977), pp. 70-71.

19. "A Short Organum," p. 201.

20. Ibid., p. 190.

21. Ibid.

22. Critics of Brecht argue about whether Brecht's alienation-effect is a series of techniques or a "mode of analysis." Stanley Mitchell suggests that in Brecht's early epic theatre, Brecht seeks a direct effect on the audience with the alienation-effect, but with the essays of the 1930s and later, the task of art for Brecht is "laying bare a 'causal network' in a specifiable and cognisable reality." In Mitchell's view, revealing the actual devices becomes a side-issue for Brecht; more important than puncturing the illusions of the theatre is to expose the workings of capitalist society. Stanley Mitchell, "From Shklovsky to Brecht: Some Preliminary Remarks Towards a History of the Politicisation of Russian Formalism," *Screen* 15 (Summer 1974): 74-81.

    Ben Brewster, on the other hand, objects to Mitchell's point of view, arguing that for Brecht, alienation-effects are "autonomous technical devices of art, not avatars of the alienation of man under capitalism." According to Brewster, Brecht's ideas of increasing the spectator's distance involve prominent techniques to create particular effects upon the audience, not the embodiment of a Marxist philosophy. See Ben Brewster, "From Shklovsky to Brecht: A Reply," *Screen* 15 (Summer 1974): 82-101.

    Stephen Heath strongly emphasizes that knowledge of Brecht and distance must be held within a political theory. Heath believes that the major weakness in most discussions of Brecht is "the reduction of distanciation to a technique," that is, distance as the simple illustration of the illusion. See Heath, "Lessons from Brecht."

    Roland Barthes also suggests that distance for Brecht is more complicated than a particular set of devices to create an awareness of the artificiality of the theatre. Barthes claims that distance in Bunraku theatre results from a discontinuity in codes. Bunraku alters the link between the character and the actor: the agents of the spectacle are visible and impassive at the same time. Discontinuity of the codes provides the distance because "quotation" reigns supreme—separate declarations. Barthes maintains that in Brechtian theatre, it is not so much an expression of the real but a signification of it, therefore it is necessary for a certain distance between signified and the signifier. See "The Dolls of Bunraku," *Diacritics* 6 (Winter 1976): 44-47; "Beyond the Empire of Signs," trans. Steven

Ungar, *Visible Language* 11 (Summer 1977): 339-54; and "Barthes on Theatre,"trans. Peter W. Mathers, in *Theatre Quarterly* 9 (Spring 1979): 25-30.

23.   Brecht, "On the Use of Music in Epic Theatre," *Schriften zum Theatre*, 1935, in *Brecht on Theatre*, p. 86.

24.   Brecht, "The Street Scene," *Versuche* 10 (essay written 1938), in *Brecht on Theatre*, p. 121.

25.   Brecht, "Short Description of a New Technique of Acting," *Brecht on Theatre*, p. 139.

26.   "A Short Organum," p. 186.

27.   Brecht, "Alienation Effects in Chinese Acting," *Schriften zum Theatre* (essay written 1936), in *Brecht on Theatre*, p. 92.

28.   Brecht, "The Street Scene," p. 125.

29.   "A Short Organum," p. 192.

30.   Victor Shklovsky, "Art as Technique," in *Russian Formalist Criticism: Four Essays*, trans. Lee T. Lemon and Marion J. Reis (Lincoln: University of Nebraska Press, 1965), p. 12.
         Eva Thompson points out that for Henri Bergson, art breaks stock responses. Like Bergson, Shklovsky says that art counteracts the habitual blindness of every-day perception; art moves phenomena into unusual contexts. See *Russian Formalism and Anglo-American New Criticism* (The Netherlands: Mouton and Co., The Hague, 1971), pp. 67-68.
         Also, as Victor Erlich points out, Shklovsky's defamiliarization is a distortion of nature by a set of devices, and Shklovsky supposedly conceives of the work of literature as the sum total of stylistic devices. See *Russian Formalism: History—Doctrine*, 3rd ed. (The Netherlands: Mouton and Co., The Hague, 1969).

31.   Victor Shklovsky, "Sterne's *Tristram Shandy:* Stylistic Commentary," in *Russian Formalist Criticism*, pp. 25-57.

32.   Silvio Gaggi, "Brecht, Pirandello, and Two Traditions of Self-Critical Art," *Theatre Quarterly* 8 (Winter 1979): 42-46.

33.   Mitchell, "From Shklovsky to Brecht," p. 76.

34.   Brecht, "The *Mother Courage* Model," *Couragemodell* 1949, in *Brecht on Theatre*, p. 219.

35.   Samuel Taylor Coleridge, *Biographia Literaria*, ed. J. Shawcross, vol. 2 (London: Oxford University Press, 1907), p. 6.

36.   Brecht, "Stage Design for the Epic Theatre," *Schriften zum Theatre* (essay written 1951), *Brecht on Theatre*, p. 233.

37.   Susan Sontag, "Theatre and Film," in *Styles of Radical Will* (New York: Farrar, Straus and Giroux, Inc., 1969), p. 121.

38.   Samuel Johnson, "Cowley," in *Lives of the English Poets*, vol. 1 (London: Oxford University Press, 1952), p. 14.

39.   "Notes on Strittmatter's Play *Katzgraben*," *Junge Kunst* (notes written 1952-1953), *Brecht on Theatre*, pp. 248-49.

40.   In Leoncavallo's opera *Pagliacci (The Strolling Players)*, Canio, the leader of the troupe, discovers that his wife, Nedda, has a lover. In a play-within-the-play, Canio plays the part of Pagliacci, actually murdering Nedda (playing the part of Columbine). While Pagliacci in the comedy laughs, the spectator knows that the character of Canio anguishes.

41. Brecht, "The *Mother Courage* Model," p. 220.

42. Ibid., p. 221.

43. Alienation without identification may not be so easy, as Eric Bentley suggests: "Brecht is perhaps overconfident in assuming that when we abandon empathy we can see 'the object in itself as it really is'.... Failing to notice the inescapability of identifications, he himself makes them unconsciously. Indeed his unconscious identification with his supposed enemies becomes a source of unintended drama." *The Life of the Drama* (New York: Atheneum, 1964), pp. 161-62.

44. Eric Bentley, *Playwright as Thinker* (New York: Meridian Books, 1946), p. 219.

45. "A Short Organum," p. 180.

Chapter 4

1.   Jerzy Grotowski, "Holiday," *The Drama Review* 17 (March 1973): 130. All subsequent references to this article will appear in parentheses in the text throughout the rest of the chapter.

2.   Grotowski, "Towards a Poor Theatre" (1965), trans. T.K. Wiewiorowski, title essay in *Towards a Poor Theatre* (New York: Simon and Schuster, 1968), p. 16.

3.   "The Theatre's New Testament," interview with Grotowski (1964), trans. Jörgen Andersen and Judy Barba, in *Towards a Poor Theatre*, p. 34.

4.   Grotowski, "Statement of Principles," trans. Maja Buszewicz and Judy Barba, in *Towards a Poor Theatre*, p. 256.

5.   The similarities between Artaud and Grotowski are especially remarkable given the fact that neither worked with nor read the writings of the other. As Raymonde Temkine points out, "Grotowski knew neither the Théâtre Alfred Jarry nor Artaud's writings. He learned of the existence of Artaud after his death, when Grotowski was already the director of the Laboratory Theatre." *Grotowski,* trans. Alex Szogyi (New York: Avon Books, 1972), p. 144.

6.   Antonin Artaud, "The Evolution of Decor" (1924), in *Selected Writings,* ed. Susan Sontag (New York: Farrar, Straus and Giroux, 1976), p. 53.

7.   Artaud, *Theatre and Its Double,* trans. Victor Corti (London: Calder and Boyars, 1970), p. 84. All subsequent references to this book will appear in parentheses in the text throughout the rest of the chapter.

8.   Artaud, "Manifesto for a Theatre That Failed" (1926) in *Selected Writings,* p. 160.

9.   "The Theatre's New Testament," pp. 41-42.

10. Grotowski, "Towards a Poor Theatre," p. 23.

11. George Wellwarth maintains that for Artaud, the functions of drama are: 1) to protest against the artificial values of culture—to strip away artificiality; and 2) to demonstrate the true reality of the human soul. See *The Theatre of Protest and Paradox: Developments in the Avant-Garde Drama* (New York: New York University Press, 1964), pp. 17-18.

12. Grotowski, "Towards a Poor Theatre," pp. 21-22.

13. Richard Schechner, *Essays on Performance Theory 1970-1976* (New York: Drama Book Specialists, 1977), p. 124.

14. Roger Copeland, "Brecht, Artaud and the Hole in the Paper Sky," *Theatre* 9 (Summer 1978): 46-48.

15. Immanuel Kant, *The Critique of Judgement,* trans. James Creed Meredith (Oxford: Clarendon Press, 1952), p. 49.

16. Ibid., pp. 43-44.

17. Significantly influenced by Artaud and other theorists advocating a reduction of distance, Bernard Beckerman provides a more balanced explanation of reduced distance, claiming that ideally the spectator's awareness of the artificial aspects of the performance is significantly reduced when experiencing the most intense illusion, "an illusion of actuality." See *Dynamics of Drama: Theory and Method of Analysis* (New York: Knopf, 1970), p. 22.

18. "Ritual" is a dangerous metaphor to employ in discussions of theatre because it can so easily slip into a literal application—as it so often has—either by its user or by a reader, or both. As Brecht has said, the interesting thing about the ritual origins of drama is that ritual and drama went their separate ways. For obvious reasons Artaud's use of "plague" has created fewer problems for readers and commentators.

19. Artaud, "The Alfred Jarry Theatre" (c. 1920s), in *Selected Writings,* pp. 156-57.

20. "The Theatre's New Testament," p. 37.

21. Peter Brook, *The Empty Space* (New York: Atheneum, 1969), p. 72.

22. Ibid., p. 90.

23. Peter Brook, "Introduction," *Tell Me Lies,* ed. Michael Kustow, Geoffrey Reeves, and Albert Hunt (New York: The Bobbs-Merrill Co., 1968), p. 11.

24. This move in Grotowski's work toward group therapy (or something like therapy) is quite evident in Richard Mennen's description of his own experience of one of Grotowski's "meetings." See "Jerzy Grotowski's Paratheatrical Projects," *The Drama Review* 19 (December 1975): 66-69. For a more negatively critical view of this socio-therapeutic experience in Grotowski's work, see Daniel E. Cashman, "Grotowski: His Twentieth Anniversary," *Theatre Journal* 31 (December 1979): 460-66.

Chapter 5

1. Christian Metz, "On the Impression of Reality in Cinema" (1968), in *Film Language: A Semiotics of the Cinema,* trans. Michael Taylor (New York: Oxford University Press, 1974), pp. 9-10.

2. Ibid., p. 11.

3. Ibid., p. 12.

4. Brian Henderson emphasizes that it is "not reality but a certain impression of reality [that] is the basis of Metz's argument." See "Metz: Essais I and Film Theory," *Film Quarterly* 28 (Spring 1975): 21.

5. Christian Metz, "The Imaginary Signifier," trans. Ben Brewster, *Screen* 16 (Summer 1975): 47. Subsequent references to this essay will appear in parentheses in the text throughout the rest of the chapter.

6. André Bazin, "Theatre and Cinema," in *What is Cinema?,* vol. I, trans. Hugh Gray (Berkeley and Los Angeles: University of California Press, 1967), p. 99. Subsequent references to this essay will appear in parentheses in the text throughout the rest of the chapter.

7. In one of his most influential essays, "The Ontology of the Photographic Image," Bazin contends that the "essentially objective character of photography" is due to the use of a "nonliving agent": "For the first time an image of the world is formed automatically, without the creative intervention of man." Though the photograph may reflect some of the photographer's personality, this is not the same as the subjective role of the painter in painting. "All the arts are based on the presence of man, only photography derives an advantage from his absence. Photography affects us like a phenomenon in nature, like a flower or a snowflake whose vegetable or earthly origins are an inseparable part of their beauty." *What is Cinema?*, vol. I., p. 13. The "realism" of film, in Bazin's view, is largely determined by the objective nature of its creation. It presumably affects us like nature due to the (relative) absence of a human creator.

8. Similarly to Bazin, Susan Sontag points out cinema's unique use of space: "If an irreducible distinction between theatre and cinema does exist, it may be this. Theatre is confined to a logical or *continuous* use of space. Cinema . . . has access to an alogical or *discontinuous* use of space. In the theatre, actors are either in the stage space or 'off.' When 'on,' they are always visible or visualizable in contiguity with each other. In the cinema, no such relation is necessarily visible or even visualizable." "Theatre and Film," in *Styles of Radical Will* (New York: Farrar, Straus and Giroux, In., 1969), p. 108.

9. Taking Jean Mitry's ideas a step further, Metz explains that the decor of the theatre is not on the same level of reality as the actor: decor is always something of a frame in theatre. In film, on the other hand, there is no decor: every element of the world of the film is on the same level of reality, creating "homogenous pseudo-worlds." See Christian Metz, "Metz on Jean Mitry's *L'Esthetique et Psychologie du Cinema*, vol. II," trans. Diana Matias, *Screen* 14 (Spring-Summer, 1973): 64.

10. Bazin, *What is Cinema?*, vol. II, trans. Hugh Gray (Berkeley and Los Angeles: University of California Press, 1971), p. 27.

11. As Bazin explains, "What we lose by way of direct witness do we not recapture thanks to the artificial proximity provided by photographic enlargement? Everything takes place as if in the time-space perimeter which is the definition of presence. The cinema offers us effectively only a measure of duration, reduced but not to zero, while the increase in the space factor reestablishes the equilibrium of the psychological equation." *What is Cinema?*, vol. I, p. 98.

12. "The Ontology of the Photographic Image," *What is Cinema?*, vol. I, pp. 13-14.

13. Because Bazin sees reality as manifesting ambiguity, he prefers those films which reveal reality's "mystery," that is, films using the "depth of focus" technique (such as Orson Wells's films), thereby restoring "to cinematographic illusion a fundamental quality of reality—its continuity." This depth of focus technique "introduces an obviously abstract element into reality" but "because we are so used to abstractions, we no longer sense them." "An Aesthetic of Reality," *What is Cinema?*, vol. II, p. 28.

    Again, though Bazin recognizes the artificial element in the creation of films, he prefers those films which produce the least awareness of those conventions and devices, thereby presumably bringing us closer to actual reality.

14. For a more detailed explanation of Lacan's "Mirror Phase" identification, see Jacques Lacan, "The Mirror-phase as Formative of the Function of the I," trans. Jean Roussel, *New Left Review* 51 (September-October, 1968): 71-77.

    For a technical (but brief) definition of "identification" in Freudian psychoanalysis, see Jean La Planche and J.-B. Pontalis, *The Language of Psycho-Analysis,* trans. Donald Nicholson Smith (New York: Norton, 1973), pp. 205-9.

15.   Lacan explains: "The fact is that the total form of the body by which the subject anticipates in a mirage the maturation of his power is only given to him as *Gestalt,* that is to say in an exteriority in which this form is certainly more constituent than constituted, but in which it appears to him above all in a contrasting size that fixes it and a symmetry that inverts it which are in conflict with the turbulence of the motions which the subject feels animating him" (p. 73). And Lacan later adds that "the *mirror-phase* is a drama whose internal impulse rushes from insufficiency to anticipation and which manufactures for the subject, captive to the lure of spatial identification, the succession of phantasies from a fragmented body-image to a form of its totality...." "Mirror-phase," p. 74.

16.   Bazin does admit that "the faithful reproduction of reality is not art" but rather consists of "selection and interpretation." "De Sica: Metteur en Scene," *What Is Cinema?,* vol. II, p. 64. But the preferable film, in Bazin's view, is not one which introduces reality into the work for some "transcendent" purpose (whether "dramatic, moral, or ideological") but one which represents reality "at the expense of dramatic structures," as in the case of Italian neorealism. "The relation between meaning and appearance [is] in a sense inverted, appearance is always presented as a unique discovery, an almost documentary revelation that retains its full force of vividness and detail. Whence the director's art lies in the skill with which he compels the event to reveal its meaning—or at least the meaning he lends it— without removing any of its ambiguity." "*Cabiria:* The Voyage to the End of Neorealism," *What is Cinema?,* vol. II, p. 87. It is in this sense that Bazin is concerned with *actual* reality: he prefers the continuity and ambiguity of actual reality to the chopped-up versions of reality (through montage) that present a particular moral, political, dramatic, or philosophical point of view. Bazin wants the film to be as close to actual reality as it can get without ceasing to be a film.

17.   Dudley Andrew insightfully explains why Bazin adopts the theory of the "inalienable realism" of film. Andrew explains that Bazin's system is determined by his world view, greatly affected by personalism and Christian existentialism. The personalist approach keeps in view the " 'mysterious otherness' of eternal reality"; and the existential point of view conceives of reality as "an 'emerging something' which the mind essentially participates in and which can be said to exist only in experience." It is for these reasons, then, that Bazin prefers films which "aid in our encounters with the fullness of the universe" rather than the more "subjective" films which merely reveal opinions through "manipulative" film-making. *André Bazin* (New York: Oxford University Press, 1978), pp. 105-7.

18.   "The Impression of Reality," pp. 13-14.

19.   Christian Metz, "The Fiction Film and Its Spectator: A Metapsychological Study," trans. Alfred Guzzetti, *New Literary History* 8 (Autumn 1976): 85.

20.   Ibid., p. 101.

21.   Metz's theory of identification is limited also to the extent that he establishes the spectator involvement in the film as a "mirror identification." Although there are certain things about film-viewing that may be somewhat similar to the child's identification with his own image (the unity of the body projected to others), fundamental differences exist between the two: the child is not consciously aware of what is happening while the spectator is conscious of the film as a film; the infant is in a primary narcissistic stage while the adult viewer has developed his or her own ego and therefore more consciously and independently responds to the film; the child sees his or her own image in the mirror while the spectator sees projected images created by another. And, as Rick Altman points out, the use of the mirror analogy is problematic in that the discourse itself is "imaginary" as "it focuses cinema's various aspects around a single constitutive metaphor..., thus providing the cinematic experience with a

unity it otherwise would lack." See Charles Altman, "Psychoanalysis and Cinema: The Imaginary Discourse," *Quarterly Review of Film Studies* 2 (Autumn 1977): 272.

In addition, Metz's analysis is problematic in its confusing description, maintaining that we identify with inanimate objects (the camera, the screen, the projector), and with ourself as perceiving subject. His use of the term "imaginary" shifts throughout the essay, at times referring to the more everyday meaning of the term ("imaginary" in the sense of the image being fictive, nonexistent, "absent"), and at other times referring to the more technical Lacanian concept of imaginary realm (during which the child, in the "mirror phase," experiences primary narcissism—that is, identification with his own image).

Unlike the child in the imaginary realm, the film spectator does not see him or herself as the camera, nor does the viewer project the unity of self onto the inanimate apparatus.

22. Jean-Louis Baudry contends that film conventions and devices have "ideological effects": "The meaning effect produced does not depend only on the content of the images but also on the material procedures by which an illusion of continuity, dependent on the persistence of vision, is restored from discontinuous elements." See "Ideological Effects of the Basic Cinematographic Apparatus," *Film Quarterly* 28 (Winter 1974-75); 42.

23. "This complicity is most evident in the films of Alfred Hitchcock, who can be seen in one sense as the epitome of the 'classical cinema.'" See Mary Ann Doane, "The Dialogical Text: Filmic Irony and the Spectator" (Ph.D. dissertation, The University of Iowa, 1979), p. 20.

24. Stephen Heath, "Narrative Space," *Screen* 17 (Autumn 1976): 97.

25. "Metz on Mitry," p. 43.

Jurij Lotman emphasizes the dual awareness of the spectator when he maintains that the film-viewer simultaneously forgets he or she is confronted with an imaginary event and does not forget it. He discusses Bergman's "Persona" in terms of how it lowers and increases an awareness of filmic conventions. "The Illusion of Reality," in *The Semiotics of Cinema,* trans. Mark Suino (The University of Michigan), reprinted in *Film Theory and Criticism,* ed. Gerald Mast and Marshall Cohen (New York: Oxford University Press, 1979), pp. 62-64.

William Earle contends that ironic films essentially creates a double awareness of action and artificial medium. See "Revolt Against Realism in the Films," *The Journal of Aesthetics and Art Criticism* 27 (Winter 1968): 150-51. (It seems, however, that this double awareness is true for all films; it is merely a matter of degrees.)

26. Doane, "The Dialogical Text," p. 15.

27. "On Dramatic Style," *Sartre on Theatre,* p. 9.

28. For an analysis of point of view in the novel, see Wayne Booth, *The Rhetoric of Fiction* (Chicago: The University of Chicago Press, 1961); for a discussion of point of view in film, see Stephen Heath's "Narrative Space."

29. A vivid example of an enforced point of view in film is when the camera focuses in on the cat toward the end of *The Alien.* By forcing the film spectator (through close-ups) to notice the cat, the animal takes on a new significance within the context of the narrative: an alien is on board the spaceship and is capable of living inside the bodies of other organisms. The spectator perceives the cat from a very specific perspective: the viewer fears that the alien is living inside the cat.

30. See chapter 6, note 18 on the reader's changing "perspectives" in the theories of Pearse and Iser.

Chapter 6

1. Roger Scruton, *Art and Imagination: A Study in the Philosophy of Mind* (London: Methuen and Co., 1974), p. 73. Subsequent references to this book will be included in parentheses in the text throughout the rest of the chapter.

2. Hans Robert Jauss attempts to break down the perceiver's (reader's) identification into five different "levels" which correspond to the various kinds of heroes found in literary works, emphasizing that the reception of the work is not simply a matter of identifying with a character, but rather a phenomenon in which the reader identifies in different ways. See "Levels of Identification of Hero and Audience," *New Literary History* 5 (Autumn 1973): 283-317; and "Interview with Hans R. Jauss" in *Diacritics* 5 (Spring 1975): 53-61.

    Although Jauss's theory is a good start for a detailed account of audience involvement, it seems too restricted to character "types" as determined by various genres. It is also important to consider the different "levels" of identification the spectator (reader) can experience while perceiving any given work by responding to different types of characters and by alternating his or her frame of reference.

3. Koestler maintains that such psychological protection allows for a "partial breakdown of the crust of personal identity" (p. 345), as we are able to project our emotions into the object outside of ourselves. The perceiver, contends Koestler, more or less forgets his or her own existence as he or she participates in the existence of the fictional characters. In Koestler's view, such identification temporarily inhibits "self-asserting tendencies," thereby leading to the experience of vicarious emotions. *The Act of Creation* (New York: Macmillan, 1964), p. 278. Koestler also maintains that "the process of identification ... is transitory and partial, confined to certain climactic moments." *Janus* (New York: Random House, 1978), p. 76.

4. In his analysis of perception Wittgenstein distinguishes between "seeing" and "seeing as," but does not apply this insight to aesthetics. Scruton and others discuss aesthetic perception as a subcategory of that class of perception referred to by Wittgenstein as "seeing as."

5. Sartre, *The Emotions: Outline of a Theory,* trans. Bernard Frechtman (New York: Philosophical Library, 1948), pp. 50-51.

6. Ibid., p. 91.

    Sartre's view that one cannot reflect upon one's emotion while at the peak of experiencing it is similar to Husserl's notion that one cannot reflect on the image until it is in the past.

7. Various theorists, most notably those in the area of Reception Aesthetics, emphasize that the work's experiential "meaning" is partially determined by the work's creation of expectation in the perceiver (reader). See Wolfgang Iser's "The Reading Process: A Phenomenological Approach," *New Literary History* 3 (Autumn 1971): 279-99; and his *The Implied Reader: Patterns of Communication in Prose Fiction from Bunyan to Beckett* (Baltimore: Johns Hopkins University Press, 1974). See also Stanley Fish, "Literature in the Reader: Affective Stylistics," *New Literary History* 2 (Autumn 1970): 123-62; and Hans Robert Jauss, "Theses on the Transition from the Aesthetics of Literary Works to a Theory of Aesthetic Experience," in *Interpretation of Narrative,* ed. Mario J. Valdés and Owen J. Miller (Buffalo: University of Toronto Press, 1978), pp. 137-47.

    And as E.H. Gombrich explains, "Artistic communication is quite unlike throwing hand grenades. There must be not only a sender but also a receiver suitably attuned. In our response to expresssion no less than in our reading of representation, our expectations of possibilities and probabilities must come into play." *Art and Illusion: A Study in the Psychology of Pictorial Representation* (Princeton, New Jersey: Princeton University Press, 1960), p. 373.

8.   Samuel Johnson, "Preface to Shakespeare" (written 1765), in *Johnson on Shakespeare*, ed. Walter Raleigh (London: Oxford University Press, 1925), pp. 27-28.

9.   Samuel Taylor Coleridge, "Lecture on Shakespeare and Milton," in *Shakespearean Criticism*, ed. Thomas Middleton Raysor, vol. 2 (New York: E.P. Dutton, 1960), p. 46.

10. The concept of tacit awareness or tacit knowledge is central to Michael Polanyi's *The Tacit Dimension* (Garden City, New York: Doubleday, 1966).
      One could say that the awareness of fictionality, and the resulting imaginative involvement, occurs when the art object is conceived to be an intentional object, that is, in the case of art, as an object or event made by a person or group of people for the purpose of creating an aesthetic experience. The work "reveals" its intentionality through its use of conventions. And though there are difficulties in viewing art works as "communication events," Sol Worth and Larry Gross explain how we might recognize the intentionality of a "symbolic event":

      The interpretation of the meaning of a symbolic event . . . is embodied in our recognition of its structure—that is, in our recognition of its possible communicational significance. In order to recognize the structure which defines a communication event—as distinguished from a natural event—we must bring to that act of recognition an assumption of intention. We must assume that the structure we recognize is, in a sense, 'made,' performed, or produced for the purpose of 'symbolizing,' or communicating ("Symbolic Strategies," *The Journal of Communication* 24 [Autumn 1974]: 27).

      We can make those assumptions of intention, Worth and Gross explain, through judgments about conventions:

      Intention is verified by conventions of social accountability, conventions of legitimacy, and rules, genres, and styles of articulation and performance. These are the bases which make our assumptions of intentionality reasonable, justifiable, social, and communicational (p. 39).

      As E.H. Gombrich points out, every mode of representation possesses a conventional element; no art is ever free of its conventions. (*Art and Illusion*, pp. 291, 298-99.) "The medium is used to express. . . . It is not an immediate expression but one dependent on conventions" (p. 374). And, as Arthur Koestler explains, the power of convention is as a hidden persuader; every work of art is governed by "selective codes which lend coherence to the artist's vision, and at the same time restrict his freedom" (*Act of Creation*, p. 376, 380).
      Erving Goffman contends that "dramatic scriptings allow for the manipulation of framing conventions and that since these conventions cut very deeply into the organization of experience, almost everything can be managed in a way that is compatible with sustaining the involvement of the audience." See *Frame Analysis: An Essay on the Organization of Experience* (New York: Harper and Row, 1974), p. 241.

11. Various theorists have explained the art experience in terms of the spectator "make-believing" with the fictional event. See David Novitz, "Fiction, Imagination and Emotion," *The Journal of Aesthetics and Art Criticism* 38 (Spring 1980): 279-88; and Eva Schaper, "Fiction and the Suspension of Disbelief," *British Journal of Aesthetics* 18 (Winter 1978): 31-44; and Kendall Walton, "Fearing Fictions," *The Journal of Philosophy* 75 (January 1978): 5-27.

12. Arthur Koestler, *The Act of Creation*, p. 301.

13. Ibid., p. 350.

14. *The Dynamics of Literary Response* (New York: Oxford University Press, 1968), p. 102. See also Holland's "Unity Identity Text Self," *PMLA* 90 (October 1975): 813-22.

15.   Brecht, like most other theorists who have written on aesthetic distance, is much concerned with the spectator's freedom, as when he describes the Epic Theatre actor's technique, which is to insure the freedom of the audience to feel independently of the characters: "He has just to show the character, or rather he has to do more than just get into it; this does not mean that if he is playing passionate parts he must himself remain cold. It is only that his feelings must not at bottom be those of the character, so that the audience's may not at bottom be those of the character either. The audience must have complete freedom here" ("The Short Organum," *Brecht on Theatre*, pp. 194-95).

It seems a limitation in the scope of his theoretical understanding that Brecht makes the spectator's freedom a consequence of radical distanciation. Brecht seems unable, or unwilling, to admit that all drama employs distance and that distance itself involves freedom, just as he is unwilling to admit that traditional drama might be capable of generating ideas in the spectator's mind. On the other hand, Grotowski makes, if anything, even more exclusive claims for a radical decrease in distance as the source of the spectator's freedom (though Grotowski also spurns "traditional" theatre for being cold, artificial and over-distanced).

16.   Roman Ingarden, *The Literary Work of Art,* trans. George Grabowicz (Evanston, Ill.: Northwestern University Press, 1973).

In a similar fashion to Ingarden, another reception aesthetician emphasizes that the perceiver (reader) is partial creator of the aesthetic object. Wolfgang Iser claims that "the convergence of text and reader brings the literary work into existence" ("The Reading Process," p. 279); in addition, he states that, "guided by the signs of the text, the reader is induced to construct the imaginary object. It follows that the involvement of the reader is essential to the fulfillment of the text, for materially speaking this exists only as a potential reality—it requires a 'subject'... for the potential to be actualized." "The Reality of Fiction: A Functionalist Approach to Literature," *New Literary History* 7 (Autumn 1975); 18.

With a similar orientation, the dramatic theorist J.L. Styan locates the play in the mind of the spectator: "A play is the response of an audience to its performance." *The Elements of Drama* (London: Cambridge University Press, 1960), p. 5. In his later work, Styan also explains that "the spectator interprets and so contributes to and finally becomes the play, whose image is all and only in his mind." *Drama, Stage and Audience*, p. 4.

17.   The variablility of these components of distance provide the basis for some definitions, of sorts, for various distance and nondistance states:

—Under normal circumstances the real has no "distance": it is perceived passively, unconsciously and as real.

—When an actor is seen as a character, this phenomenon is what we might call "normal" aesthetic distance, embracing a wide range of drama, including fantasy as well as naturalistic plays.

—Increased distance is consistent with the perception of the actor as an actor (involving increased awareness of the conventional nature of theatre, awareness of fictionality, and awareness of the conditional mode of belief).

—When the character only is seen, all awareness of fiction lost, there is a loss of distance, what might be called delusion or hypnosis.

—When the actor is seen as a person (not as an actor), then there is a complete loss of distance; as Sartre says, when the actor seems to be looking at and into the spectator, he becomes a person who threatens the spectator's privacy.

18.   Another way of describing the spectator's varying degrees of distance is to emphasize the changing perspectives or "roles" of the spectator or reader. James A. Pearse maintains that

twentieth-century "metafiction differs from traditional fiction through its manipulations in narrative perspectives.... Metafiction forces the reader out of traditional narrational frames.... In metafiction, the act of performance itself keys the unveiling of the narrative perspective." "Beyond the Narrational Frame: Interpretation and Metafiction," *The Quarterly Journal of Speech* 66 (February 1980); 74-75.

In *The Implied Reader,* Iser maintains that the "role" of the reader changes historically, with the twentieth century creating an "even more complex role because the reader is apparently forced to be more self-aware, more observant of his or her own reading process and thought patterns" (p. xiv). In his later essay, Iser more specifically deals with this notion of shifting perspectives, maintaining that combined within the narrative is "a whole system of perspectives," the interaction between which is continuous. "Narrative Strategies as a Means of Communication," in *Interpretation of Narrative,* ed. Mario J. Valdés and Owen J. Miller (Buffalo: University of Toronto, 1978), p. 111.

19.   Bethell maintains that in Shakespearean plays, the mixture of comedy and tragedy relies on the audience's ability to quickly adjust their mode of attention, thereby exercising their "multi-consciousness" in temporal succession. *Shakespeare and the Popular Dramatic Tradition,* p. 108.

Bibliography

Albee, Edward. "An Interview with Edward Albee." In *The American Theatre Today*, edited by Alan S. Downer. New York: Basic Books, Inc., 1967, pp. 111-23.

Aldritch, Virgil C. "Back to Aesthetic Experience." *The Journal of Aesthetics and Art Criticism* 24 (Spring 1966): 365-72.

Altman, Charles F. "Psychoanalysis and Cinema: The Imaginary Discourse." *Quarterly Review of Film Studies* 2 (August 1977): 257-72.

Andrew, Dudley. *André Bazin*. New York: Oxford University Press, 1978.

Aristotle. *Aristotle's Theory of Poetry and Fine Art*. Translated by S.H. Butcher. 4th ed. London: Macmillan and Co., 1922.

_____. *Metaphysics*. Translated by W.D. Ross. 2nd ed. Oxford: Clarendon Press, 1928.

_____. *Nicomachian Ethics*. Translated by H. Rackham. New York: G.P. Putnam's Sons, 1934.

Artaud, Antonin. *Collected Works*. Translated by Victor Corti. 4 vols. London: Calder and Boyars, 1971-1974.

_____. *Selected Writings*. Edited by Susan Sontag. New York: Farrar, Straus and Giroux, 1976.

_____. *Theatre and Its Double*. Translated by Victor Corti. London: Calder and Boyars, 1970.

Barthes, Roland. "Barthes on Theatre." Translated by Peter W. Mathers. *Theatre Quarterly* 9 (Spring 1979): 25-30.

_____. "Beyond the Empire of Signs." Translated by Steven Ungar. *Visible Language* 11 (Summer 1977): 339-54.

_____. "Diderot, Brecht, Eisenstein." In *Image—Music—Text*. Translated by Stephen Heath. New York: Hill and Wang, 1977, pp. 69-78.

_____. "The Dolls of Bunraku." *Diacritics* 6 (Winter 1976): 44-47.

Baudry, Jean-Louis. "Ideological Effects of the Basic Cinematographic Apparatus." *Film Quarterly* 28 (Winter 1974-75): 39-47.

Bazin, André. *What is Cinema?* Vol. I. Translated by Hugh Gray. Berkeley and Los Angeles: University of California Press, 1967.

_____. *What is Cinema?* Vol II. Translated by Hugh Gray. Berkeley and Los Angeles: University of California Press, 1971.

Beardsley, Monroe C. "Aesthetic Experience Regained." *The Journal of Aesthetics and Art Criticism* 28 (Fall 1969); 3-11.

Beckerman, Bernard. *Dynamics of Drama: Theory and Method of Analysis*. New York: Knopf, 1970.

Bentley, Eric. *The Life of the Drama*. New York: Atheneum, 1964.

_____. *The Playwright as Thinker*. New York: Meridian Books, Inc., 1946.

Bergson, Henri. *Laughter: An Essay on the Meaning of the Comic*. Translated by Cloudesley Brereton and Fred Rothwell. New York: Macmillan, 1924.

Bethell, Samuel L. *Shakespeare and the Popular Dramatic Tradition*. Westminster: Staples Press Limited, 1944.

Booth, Wayne C. *The Rhetoric of Fiction.* Chicago: The University of Chicago Press, 1961.

Brecht, Bertolt. *Brecht on Theatre.* Edited and translated by John Willett. New York: Hill and Wang, 1964.

Brewster, Ben. "From Shklovsky to Brecht: A Reply." *Screen* 15 (Summer 1974): 82-101.

Brook, Peter. *The Empty Space.* New York: Atheneum, 1969.

——. "Introduction." In *Tell Me Lies,* edited by Michael Kustow, Geoffrey Reeves, and Albert Hunt. New York: The Bobbs-Merrill Company, 1968.

Bukala, C.R. "Sartre's Dramatic Philosophical Quest." *Thought* 48 (Spring 1973): 79-106.

Bullough, Edward. "'Phychical Distance' as a Factor in Art and an Aesthetic Principle." *British Journal of Psychology* 5 (June, 1912): 87-118.

Casebier, Allan. "The Concept of Aesthetic Distance." *The Personalist,* Winter, 1971, pp. 70-91. Reprinted in *Aesthetics: A Critical Anthology,* edited by George Dickie and Richard J. Sclafani. New York: St. Martin's Press, 1977, pp. 783-99.

Cashman, Daniel E. "Grotowski: His Twentieth Anniversary." *Theatre Journal* 31 (December 1979): 460-66.

Cohen, Marshall. "Appearance and the Aesthetic Attitude." *The Journal of Philosophy* 56 (November 1959): 915-26.

Coleridge, Samuel Taylor. *Biographia Literaria.* Edited by J. Shawcross. Vol. 2. London: Oxford University Press, 1907.

——. *Shakespearean Criticism.* Edited by Thomas Middleton Raysor. Vol. 2. New York: E.P. Dutton, 1960.

Copeland, Roger. "Brecht, Artaud and the Hole in the Paper Sky." *Theatre* 9 (Summer 1978): 42-49.

Crossley, D.J. "The Aesthetic Attitude: Back in Gear with Bullough." *The Personalist* 56 (Summer 1975): 336-45.

Dickie, George. *Aesthetics: An Introduction.* Indianapolis: Bobbs-Merrill, 1971.

——. "Attitude and Object: Aldrich on the Aesthetic." *The Journal of Aesthetics and Art Criticism* 25 (Fall 1966): 89-91.

——. "Beardsley's Phantom Aesthetic Experience." *The Journal of Philosophy* 63 (March 1965): 129-36.

——. "Bullough and Casebier: Disappearing in the Distance." *The Personalist* 53 (1972): 127-31.

——. "Bullough and the Concept of Psychical Distance." *Philosophy and Phenomenological Research* 22 (December 1961): 233-38.

——. "Is Psychology Relevant to Aesthetics?" *Philosophical Review* 71 (July 1962): 285-302.

——. "The Myth of the Aesthetic Attitude." *American Philosophical Quarterly* 1 (January 1964). Reprinted in *Introductory Readings in Aesthetics,* edited by John Hospers. New York: The Free Press, 1969, pp. 28-44.

Doane, Mary Ann. "The Dialogical Text: Filmic Irony and the Spectator." Ph.D. dissertation, The University of Iowa, 1979.

Ducasse, Curt John. *The Philosophy of Art,* Chapter 9, "The Aesthetic Attitude." New York: Dial Press, 1929, pp. 134-50.

Earle, William. "Revolt Against Realism in the Films." *The Journal of Aesthetics and Art Criticism* 27 (Winter 1968): 145-51.

Erlich, Victor. *Russian Formalism: History—Doctrine.* 3rd ed. The Netherlands: Mouton and Company, The Hague, 1969.

Fish, Stanley. "Literature in the Reader: Affective Stylistics." *New Literary History* 2 (Autumn 1970): 123-62.

Gaggi, Silvio. "Brecht, Pirandello, and Two Traditions of Self-Critical Art." *Theatre Quarterly* 8 (Winter 1979): 42-46.

Goffman, Erving. *Frame Analysis: An Essay on the Organization of Experience.* New York: Harper and Row, 1974.

Gombrich, E.H. *Art and Illusion: A Study in the Psychology of Pictorial Representation.* Princeton, New Jersey: Princeton University Press, 1960.

Grotowski, Jerzy. "Holiday." *The Drama Review* 17 (March 1973): 113-35.

_____. *Towards a Poor Theatre.* New York: Simon and Schuster, 1968.

Hampton, Charles C. Jr. "Verfremcluhanseffkt." *Modern Drama* 14 (December 1971): 340-54.

Heath, Stephen. "Lessons from Brecht." *Screen* 15 (Summer 1974): 103-28.

_____. "Narrative Space." *Screen* 17 (Autumn 1976): 68-112.

Henderson, Brian. "Metz: Essais I and Film Theory." *Film Quarterly* 28 (Spring 1975): 18-33.

Holland Norman. *The Dynamics of Literary Response.* New York: Oxford University Press, 1968.

_____. *5 Readers Reading.* New Haven: Yale University Press, 1975.

_____. "Unity Identity Text Self." *PMLA* 90 (October 1975): 813-22.

Ingarden, Roman. *The Literary Work of Art.* Translated by George Grabowicz. Evanston, Illinois: Northwestern University Press, 1973.

Iser, Wolfgang. *The Implied Reader: Patterns of Communication in Prose Fiction from Bunyan to Beckett.* Baltimore: Johns Hopkins University Press, 1974.

_____. "Narrative Strategies as a Means of Communication." In *Interpretation of Narrative,* edited by Mario J. Valdés and Owen J. Miller. Buffalo: University of Toronto Press, 1978, pp. 100-117.

_____. "The Reading Process: A Phenomenological Approach." *New Literary History* 3 (Autumn 1971): 279-99.

_____. "The Reality of Fiction: A Functionalist Approach to Literature." *New Literary History* 7 (Autumn 1975): 6-38.

James, William. *The Principles of Psychology.* Vol. 1. New York: Henry Holt and Co., 1890.

Jauss, Hans Robert. "Interview with Hans R. Jauss." *Diacritics* 5 (Spring 1975): 53-61.

_____. "Levels of Identification of Hero and Audience." *New Literary History* 5 (Autumn 1973): 283-317.

_____. "Theses on the Transition from the Aesthetics of Literary Works to a Theory of Aesthetic Experience." in *Interpretation of Narrative,* edited by Mario J. Valdés and Owen J. Miller. Buffalo: University of Toronto Press, 1978, pp. 137-47.

Johnson, Samuel. "Cowley." In *Lives of the English Poets.* Vol. 1. London: Oxford University Press, 1952, pp. 1-53.

_____. "Preface to Shakespeare." In *Johnson on Shakespeare,* edited by Walter Raleigh. London: Oxford University Press, 1925, pp. 9-63.

Kaelin, Eugene F. *An Existentialist Aesthetic: The Theories of Sartre and Merleau-Ponty.* Madison: The University of Wisconsin Press, 1962.

Kant, Immanuel. *The Critique of Judgement.* Translated by James Creed Meredith. Oxford: Clarendon Press, 1952.

Kelley, Harold H. "The Processes of Causal Attribution." *American Psychologist* 28 (February 1973): 107-28.

Koestler, Arthur. *The Act of Creation.* New York: Macmillan, 1964.

_____. *Janus.* New York: Random House, 1978.

Lacan, Jacques. "The Mirror-phase as formative of the Function of the I." Translated by Jean Roussel. *New Left Review* 51 (September-October 1968): 71-77.

Langer, Susanne K. *Feeling and Form: A Theory of Art.* New York: Charles Scribner's Sons, 1953.

_____. *Philosophy in a New Key: A Study in the Symbolism of Reason, Rite, and Art.* 3rd ed. Cambridge, Mass.: Harvard University Press, 1957.

La Planche, Jean and J.-B. Pontalis. *The Language of Psycho-Analysis.* Translated by Donald Nicholson-Smith. New York: Norton, 1973.

Lotman, Jurij. "The Illusion of Reality." In *The Semiotics of Cinema,* translated by Mark Suino. Reprinted in *Film Theory and Criticism,* edited by Gerald Mast and Marshall Cohen. New York: Oxford University Press, 1979, pp. 55-70.

Markus, Thomas B. "Tiny Alice and Tragic Catharsis." *Educational Theatre Journal* 17 (October 1965): 225-33.

Mennen, Richard. "Jerzy Grotowski's Paratheatrical Projects." *The Drama Review* 19 (December 1975): 58-69.

Merleau-Ponty, Maurice. *The Phenomenology of Perception.* Translated by Colin Smith. New York: The Humanities Press, 1962.

Metz, Christian. "Christian Metz on Jean Mitry's L'Esthétique et Psychologie du Cinéma, vol. II." Translated by Diana Matias. *Screen* 14 (Spring-Summer 1973): 40-87.

———. "The Fiction Film and Its Spectator: A Metapsychological Study." Translated by Alfred Guzzetti. *New Literary History* 8 (Autumn 1976): 75-105.

———. "The Imaginary Signifier." Translated by Ben Brewster. *Screen* 16 (Summer 1975): 14-76.

———. "On the Impression of Reality in Cinema." In *Film Language: A Semiotics of the Cinema,* translated by Michael Taylor. New York: Oxford University Press, 1974, pp. 3-15.

Mitchell, Stanley. "From Shklovsky to Brecht: Some Preliminary Remarks Towards a History of the Politicisation of Russian Formalism." *Screen* 15 (Summer 1974): 74-81.

Nietzsche, Friedrich. *The Complete Works of Friedrich Nietzsche.* Edited by Oscar Levy. Vol. 13: *Genealogy of Morals, Peoples and Countries,* translated by H.B. Samuel. London: George Allen and Unwin, 1910.

Novitz, David. "Fiction, Imagination and Emotion." *The Journal of Aesthetics and Art Criticism* 38 (Spring 1980): 279-88.

Pearse, James A. "Beyond the Narrational Frame: Interpretation and Metafiction." *The Quarterly Journal of Speech* 66 (February 1980): 73-84.

Polanyi, Michael. *The Tacit Dimension.* Garden City, New York: Doubleday, 1966.

Reiss, Timothy J. "Psychical Distance and Theatrical Distancing in Sartre's Drama." *Yale French Studies* 46 (1971): 5-16.

Sartre, Jean-Paul. "Beyond Bourgeois Theatre." Translated by Rima Drell Reck. *The Tulane Drama Review* 5 (March 1961):3-11.

———. *The Emotions: Outline of a Theory.* Translated by Bernard Frechtman. New York: Philosophical Library, 1948.

———. *Imagination.* Translated by Forrest Williams. Ann Arbor: The University of Michigan Press, 1962.

———. "Myth and Reality in the Theatre." In *Tell Me Lies,* edited by Michael Kustow, Geoffrey Reeves, and Albert Hunt. Indianapolis and New York: The Bobbs-Merrill Co., 1968, pp. 199-201.

———. *The Psychology of Imagination.* New York: Philosophical Library, 1948.

———. *Saint Genet: Actor and Martyr.* Translated by Bernard Frechtman. New York: George Braziller, Inc., 1963.

———. *Sartre on Theatre.* Translated by Frank Jellinek. Edited by Michel Contat and Michel Rybalka. New York: Pantheon Books, 1976.

Schaper, Eva. "Fiction and the Suspension of Disbelief." *British Journal of Aesthetics* 18 (Winter 1978): 31-44.

Schopenhauer, Arthur. *The World as Will and Idea.* Translated by R.B. Haldane and John Kemp. New York: Humanities Press, 1964.

Schechner, Richard. *Essays on Performance Theory 1970-1976.* New York: Drama Book Specialists, 1977.

Schlegel, August Wilhelm von. *Course of Lectures on Dramatic Art and Literature.* Translated by John Black. London: Henry G. Bohn, 1846.

Scruton, Roger. *Art and Imagination: A Study in the Philosophy of Mind.* London: Methuen and Co., 1974.

Shaftesbury, Lord (Anthony Ashley Cooper). *Characteristics of Men, Manners, Opinions, Times, etc.* Edited by John M. Robertson. 2 vols. Gloucester, Mass.: Peter Smith, 1963.

Shklovsky, Victor. "Art as Technique" and "Sterne's *Tristram Shandy:* Stylistic Commentary." In *Russian Formalist Criticism: Four Essays,* translated by Lee T. Lemon and Marion J. Reis. Lincoln: University of Nebraska Press, 1965, pp. 3-57.

Sibley, Frank. "Aesthetics and the Looks of Things." *The Journal of Philosophy* 56 (November 1959): 905-15.

Sontag, Susan. *Against Interpretation.* New York: Farrar, Straus and Giroux, 1966.

_____. *Styles of Radical Will.* New York: Farrar, Straus and Giroux, 1969.

Steer, W.A.J. "Brecht's Epic Theatre: Theory and Practice." *The Modern Language Review* 63 (July 1968): 636-49.

Stolnitz, Jerome. *Aesthetics and Philosophy of Art Criticism.* Boston: Houghton Mifflin, 1960.

_____. "'Beauty': Some Stages in the History of an Idea." *Journal of the History of Ideas* 22 (April-June, 1961): 185-204.

_____. "Of the Origins of 'Aesthetic Disinterestedness.'" *The Journal of Aesthetics and Art Criticism* 20 (Winter 1961): 131-43.

_____. "On Artistic Familiarity and Aesthetic Value." *The Journal of Philosophy* 53 (April 1956): 261-76.

_____. "On Esthetic Valuing and Evaluation." *Philosophy and Phenomenological Research* 13 (June 1953): 467-76.

_____. "On the Formal Structure of Esthetic Theory." *Philosophy and Phenomenological Research* 12 (March 1952): 346-64.

_____. "On Ugliness in Art." *Philosophy and Phenomenological Research* 11 (September 1950): 1-24.

_____. "Some Questions Concerning Aesthetic Perception." *Philosophy and Phenomenological Research* 22 (1961-1962): 69-87.

_____. "A Third Note on Eighteenth-Century 'Disinterestedness.'" *The Journal of Aesthetics and Art Criticism* 22 (Fall 1963): 69-70.

Styan, J.L. *Drama, Stage and Audience.* London: Cambridge University, 1975.

_____. *The Elements of Drama.* London: Cambridge University, 1960.

Temkine, Raymonde. *Grotowski.* Translated by Alex Szogyi. New York: Avon Books, 1972.

Thompson, Ewa M. *Russian Formalism and Anglo-American New Criticism.* The Netherlands: Mouton and Co., The Hague, 1971.

Tomas, Vincent. "Aesthetic Vision." *Philosophical Review* 68 (1959): 52-67.

Vicentini, Claudio. "Pirandello, Stanislavsky, Brecht, and the 'Opposition Principle.'" *Modern Drama* 20 (December 1977): 381-92.

Vivas, Eliseo. *The Artistic Transaction.* Columbus, Ohio: Ohio State University Press, 1963.

_____. "A Definition of the Esthetic Experience." *The Journal of Philosophy* 34 (November 1937): 628-34.

Wallace, Robert. "*The Zoo Story:* Albee's Attack on Fiction." *Modern Drama* 16 (June 1973): 49-54.

Walton, Kendall. "Fearing Fictions." *The Journal of Philosophy.* 75 (January 1978): 5-27.

Warnock, Mary. *Imagination.* Berkeley: University of California, 1976.

Wixson, Douglas Charles Jr. "The Dramatic Techniques of Thornton Wilder and Bertolt Brecht: A Study in Comparison." *Modern Drama* 15 (May 1972): 112-24.

Woodland, Ronald S. "The Danger of Empathy in *Mother Courage.*" *Modern Drama* 15 (May 1972): 125-29.

Worth, Sol and Larry Gross. "Symbolic Strategies." *The Journal of Communication* 24 (Autumn 1974): 27-39.

Index